Helpline for Stressed Parents

Published by :
Lotus Press Publishers & Distributors

Helpline for Stressed Parents

Eric Belle

Lotus PRESS

4735/22, Prakash Deep Building
Ansari Road, Darya Ganj,
New Delhi - 110002

Lotus Press : Publishers & Distributors
Unit No. 220, 2nd Floor, 4735/22, Prakash Deep Building,
Ansari Road, Darya Ganj, New Delhi- 110002
Ph.: 23280047, 98118-38000
• E-mail : lotuspress1984@gmail.com
www.lotuspress.co.in

Helpline for Stressed Parents

ISBN: 978-81-8382-338-8

Printed & Published by : **Lotus Press Publisher & Distributors,** New Delhi-02

PREFACE

This highly materialistic world necessitates one to plunge into a cut-throat competition in every walk of life. New generation is not patient enough to weigh the pros and cons of a decision, even if it is taken in a huff. Most of them want to make a quick buck. Very often, they bite the dust. Incessant failures enable such people to withstand the vagaries of life. The modern trend of doing many-a-thing at a time fails one to use one's faculties in a proper manner. Modern technology, to a large extent, arrests one's natural capacity to stand upto the challenges and tasks of life.

The very purpose of this book is to serve as a helpline for stressed patients and all other people who are undergoing or about to fall into the menace of tension or stress.

—Author

CONTENTS

1

CHILDCARE

A tiny hand clasping the finger of a large hand—it is a familiar image. An image of infancy that evokes the baby's vulnerability and trust, and the adult's gentleness and responsibility. This is an image of caring behind the image is a story of family and societal choices. Do the baby's mother and father hold jobs? What were their options for returning to work or staying with their newborn?

Perhaps the large hand belongs not to a parent but to a teacher in a childcare centre, a neighbour who takes children into her home, or the baby's grand-mother. Who else is nearby in the care setting? Are other large hands reaching out to hold the baby, or are other small hands reaching up for the adult?

This chapter is about the care of the nation's youngest children, those who have not yet turned three. As used here, the term "care" encompasses a rainbow of different care settings and caring individuals—parents and grand-parents, nannies and neighbours, family childcare providers and childcare centres. The chapter compares our understanding of the care-giving that babies need with the capacity of today's parents to ensure that those needs are met day after day.

Why focus just on children under age three? The decision is controversial. Because development is continuous, categories based on age can be artificial and misleading. Nevertheless, the "under-threes" have been singled out in recent years. Sparked by the Carnegie Corporation's *Starting Points* report in 1994 and spurred by newly popularised research on brain development, media attention to infants and toddlers surged during the 1990s.

Amidst the excitement, some exaggerated claims were made about the uniqueness of the first years of life, prompting the National Academy of Sciences to caution that the focus on the period from birth to age three *"begins too late and ends too early."* We agree. No claim is made here that development stops or even pauses at a child's third birthday party. Instead, we distinguish this age group because the responsibility for children who are still so dependent and vulnerable poses unique demands on caregivers and care settings. A baby depends utterly on his or her caregiver to make the vast world safe, manageable, and welcoming. To share the care of a child who cannot yet walk or talk carries special meaning and weight for all involved.

All the same, the special character of the earliest years of life confounds policy-makers, professionals, and the public. What is the best care that is feasible to provide to infants and toddlers, now that more than half of America's babies have a mother who works outside the home? There are over 11 million children under age three in the United States, and this year nearly 5 million of them will spend about 25 hours a week in the care of someone other than a parent. This is a revolution in care-giving, and it leaves Americans uneasy. Is there a single desirable balance between care by parents and by others, or are there many appropriate solutions?

Parental decisions regarding both employment and childcare reflect the family's circumstances and preferences, to be sure, but public attitudes, employer policies, and government programmes also influence them. By improving the care-giving options available to families, society can support the well-being of both families and children—if we can come to agreement on our goals and priorities. That is the terrain covered in this chapter.

In emphasising the balance families strike between employment and care-giving, this chapter leaves out many aspects of care that shape infants' development. Mentioned but not discussed in detail are economic supports, health care, early intervention services for infants with developmental delays or disabilities, parent education and support programmes, and the child welfare system that steps in when parental care is inadequate. These are important services, critical to the well-being of many children.

Two reports included in this issue, one by Levine and Smith and one by Bodenhorn and Kelch, describe innovative efforts to strengthen and integrate health, parenting, and child development services. However, these allied service systems have been addressed in earlier issues of *The Future of Children*, and they are not examined again here. Instead, this issue focuses on the question of whether enough is being done to support the everyday care-giving on which infants and toddlers rely so trustingly.

This chapter opens with a brief look at the dramatic, multifaceted development that takes place during infancy, and highlights the influence that care-giving has on development. It discusses how care-giving has changed in the last half-century, with increasing maternal employment and use of non-familial childcare, and it reviews the ambivalence of public reactions to these shifts. Finally, the chapter closely at the adequacy of family leave and childcare subsidy policies designed to help American families manage the demands of work and care-giving.

It argues that further action by government, employers, and community institutions is needed to strengthen all the care-giving options families use, to ensure that a nurturing environment surrounds every young child's development.

The dramatic moment of childbirth ends with a new life being separated from its mother who nurtured and sheltered the baby during its development. When the cord is cut, the vulnerable newborn is then handed to the excited parents. However, another separation of this fragile new life from its mother is not far away. More and more in America, before this child is one year old (and often within only a few weeks) the baby will probably be in the care of someone other than its parents for about 10 hours a day.

The majority of childcare providers strive to provide services that are stimulating, safe, and nurturing. However, in some circumstances, the environment is less than optimal. Such environments can not only adversely impact the health of this exquisitely sensitive life, but in their extreme, stagnate the child's development, and fail to optimally prepare this baby for a productive life. Despite what has been learned about the real needs of developing children during the critical early years of life, there are not yet enough stable, stimulating, healthy, and loving childcare environments for all the young children who need them.

In the last two decades, more mothers and single fathers of infants and toddlers have joined the workforce. In 1970, only 30 per cent of children needed childcare. By the year 2000, an estimated 75 per cent of children under age 5 years will need childcare. For the nearly 13 million preschool children with working mothers today, good childcare is hard to find and often when found may not be accessible or may be beyond the parents' ability to pay.

Most parents find themselves on their own in locating and evaluating childcare, and again in paying for it. Because family finances must often drive decisions, many children receive less than optimal childcare that may not provide for their emotional, intellectual, social, and physical development, particularly for children with complex physical or emotional needs.

The shortage of high-quality, safe, and healthy childcare exists because this industry in the U.S. has not yet been able to catch up with the sociological changes and new needs emerging over the last few decades. The nation's $264 billion investment in children aged 6 years and older is matched by a mere $1 billion investment in those aged 5 years and younger. This dilemma has been called a "quiet crisis" by a Carnegie Foundation report that examined the health and welfare of young children in America.

The sociological change of working mothers in the United States is compounded by many other challenges. There are fewer intact families, more geographic mobility, more divorces, more violence and illegal drug use, and less support from extended families and communities. About one-fourth of pre-schoolers live in single-parent families.

These changes have reshaped the healthcare and childcare needs of young children. The current problems in childcare have not been fully recognised. Experts caution that the need for quality childcare will soon become even more acute since welfare reform legislation enacted in 1996 will require more mothers of young children to work. *The Children's Defence Fund* estimates that there are 4.5 million children under age 5 in families receiving welfare.

There are many signals that the overall health of American children is less than optimal. However, recognising this, it is also important to acknowledge that resources and opportunities exist to improve this situation. Experience with early childhood vaccinations in some model programmes provide an example of just how much impact good childcare programmes can have on the health of our children. Despite knowledge about the value of immunisations, the rates of vaccination among two-year-olds in some states in 1992 were only 30 per cent; in most states, the rates were below 60 per cent. 5 Licensed childcare programmes achieve vaccination rates of more than 90 per-cent, illustrating the potential for improvement.

Other evidence exists to support the value of health and wellness in childcare. Besides helping to improve the developmental outcomes of children quality, early childhood care and education can successfully prepare "at-risk" children for schools. It has been demonstrated that quality childcare is associated with higher IQ scores, more successful academic experiences, less adolescent delinquency, and more productive lives as adults.

Advocates for early childhood services have suggested that the United States should follow the models of other nations that support quality experiences and care in the first 5 years of life, provide parents with subsidised childcare solutions and permit longer, partially paid leaves for parents following birth.

HUMAN PROMISE OF INFANCY

Vivid images of early development have captured the attention of the media, policy-makers, and the general public. Recently, the most striking have been brightly coloured reproductions of brain scans showing dramatic differences between the brains of children exposed to terrible or positive environments during the first years of their lives. The article by Thompson in this chapter adds depth to these images by describing the captivating behaviours of babies and toddlers as they master new skills and understanding, delighting their caregivers.

Thompson emphasises that early development is designed to yield a well-rounded human being, as he explains that growth during the first three years of life transforms the infant's brain but his or her body, mind, and person. While millions of synapses are forming and being pruned in the "biologically exuberant" growing brain, the infant is also learning to decipher and speak an elaborate native language, figuring out how the physical world works, coordinating a complex set of growing muscles and bones, and discovering how to harness the dynamism of emotions and relationships with others. The early years lay the foundation for the child's later cognitive achievements, mastery of social skills, and emerging sense of self-esteem and respect for others.

While early learning looks natural and unremarkable, its significance should not be under-estimated. Physical, intellectual, and social learning occur together as a baby and caregiver go through the day's routine—talking, exploring, playing, and cuddling. Thompson's article points out that important aspects of social and emotional mastery such as curiosity, task persistence, adaptability, and self-control take root in the rich soil of these early experiences. As a committee of scholars at the *National Academy of Sciences* wrote in a 2000 report, the first years of life set "either a sturdy or fragile stage" on which the child builds the intellectual and academic skills that will be called on in school and other life contexts.

School readiness investments should encompass supports for the healthy, well-rounded development of infants and toddlers, who are mastering the social, emotional, and cognitive skills required for success in school and beyond.

The process of development, scientists agree, intertwines genetic factors, inborn forces of maturation and growth, and responsiveness to both environment and experience. In other words, nature powers much of early development, but its course depends heavily on the experiences and protections that caregivers provide. The infant's caregivers—the parents and others who are responsible for the child's routine care and overall well-being, determine many influences that shape development.

In Thompson's words, "the irreducible core of the environment of early development is people." Caregivers provide food and physical safety; they nurture and reassure the infant; they provoke and respond to the toddler's overtures; they offer playthings and challenges; and they surround the child with language.

These caregiver actions are remarkably natural, argues Thompson, although attentive care-giving cannot be taken for granted. Common problems that impede care-giving include depression and stress that may be rooted in the adult's own experiences as a child or caused by more immediate life problems. Infant-care-giver relationships are also disrupted when competing demands pull caregivers away either physically or psychologically.

Therefore, Thompson calls on society to value the caregivers who mean so much to infants, for instance, by ensuring that welfare and employment policies permit parents to remain home during the months after a child's birth, and by providing better training and more compensation to caregivers outside the family. Similarly, the article by Knitzer in this issue urges federal and state governments to invest more in programmes like Early Head Start that help vulnerable caregivers forge positive relationships with the children who depend on them.

The essence of care-giving that supports child development is a relationship with an adult who is both attentive and responsive to the infants or toddler's concerns, discoveries, and achievements. It is people who matter the most to babies.

Impacts on young children's access to attentive, nurturing care should be a key criterion when policy-makers and advocates judge policies that affect adults with care-giving responsibilities.

NEW CONFIGURATIONS OF CARE-GIVING

Caregivers and care-giving environments matter to the development of babies and toddlers—psychological science speaks clearly on that point. Sociologists, economists, and demographers weigh in on the topic as well, because among the most striking sociological changes of the last 50 years is the transformation of care-giving within families. Mothers, and particularly mothers of very young children, have entered the labour force in a growing tide.

The article by Phillips and Adams in this chapter reports that 61 per cent of American mothers with a child under age three were employed in 2000, compared with only 34 per cent in 1975. Today, work enters into the relationship between mother and baby very early. In 2000, report Phillips and Adams, 56 per cent of mothers with a baby under age one were employed. In the wake of that shift, parents have orchestrated a myriad of alternative arrangements to care for their children during work hours.

According to Phillips and Adams, a major multisite study of families found that for three of four babies, some form of non-parental childcare began during the first year of life—often as early as three months of age. Although for many infants, childcare means staying with a grandmother, the proportion of children under age three who spend their days in childcare centres has almost tripled in the last 20 years, rising from only 8 per cent to 22 per cent.

Taken together, increasing maternal employment and the growing reliance on childcare add up to what Phillips and Adams call "a dramatic reapportioning of care" away from parents to a variety of other care-givers.

Although the change in care-giving has been steady and gradual, it has attracted notice by the American public. Attentive care should be every child's birthright—about that there is little debate, but heated discussions arise over how to provide such care for babies in the face of women's growing professionalism and importance as family breadwinners. There is no consensus about the balance between parental employments and care-giving that is right for all families. No experts have offered a winning vision of how to accommodate work and family, and parents have not joined hands to press employers or Government for family-friendly policies. Why not? A closer examination of recent trends and public values concerning family self-sufficiency, care-giving, and the role of Government's offer a partial explanation.

SHOULD MOTHERS WORK?

Rates of employment among mothers of children under age three have risen consistently during the last half-century and they show no signs of slackening. Sociologists offer different explanations for the employment trends: work requirements imposed on welfare recipients, the eroding wages of men, women's response to the growing risk of divorce, women's career aspirations, and modern-day materialism. Very few experts suggest that significant numbers of women will turn their backs on employment, however. Rather, women are returning to work earlier than ever after childbirth—most by the third month.

The impact of a mother's wages on the family's budget is a persuasive factor in many households. In two-parent families, mothers contribute about one-third of the family's income. The Congressional Research Service reports that, in 1997, the median income for two-parent families with a non-working wife was $36,027, whereas families with two working parents earned $60,669. And one economic trend analysis of changing family incomes during the turbulent 1970s and 1980s revealed that a mother's income played an important role in stabilising the family's standard of living in the face of economic uncertainty.

Moreover, families with new babies tend to be young, and vulnerable economically. Although statistics are seldom reported on children under age three, 22 per cent of children under age six lived below the poverty line in 1997 (set that year at about $13,000 for a family of three), and nearly one-third did not live with both parents. In families that struggle with poverty, as has long been the case, maternal employment is taken for granted.

American attitudes toward maternal employment have been surprisingly unaffected by the rising proportions of mothers in the labour force. A flood of recent polls and surveys summarised in the article by Sylvester in this chapter shows that by margins of three or four to one, Americans continue to believe that it is best if a parent is at home to care for very young children. From an international perspective, the American ideal of the stay-at-home mother seems out of step with the times. In most European countries, maternal employment has been accepted for much of the twentieth century, and it is now expected after a child is a year old. (As Waldfogel points out, most European countries offer paid parental leave for a year after a birth.)

In the United States and other English-speaking nations, however, the public has resisted the norm of maternal employment, especially during the first years of life. Here, public reactions to parents' decisions to work and use childcare sometimes suggest that materialism and concern with status have overshadowed more fundamental family values. As one sociologist put it: "Working mothers, especially mothers of pre-schoolers, still face mixed responses among the American public who, although affirming their legal right to work, remain divided about the wisdom of and reasons for so many young mothers in the labour force. Are they working because they need to or just because they want to buy more things?"

When the topic is single, mothers and welfare policy, however, public attitudes about good parenting and employment reverse sharply. In what strikes some as a double standard, poor mothers are praised not for remaining home with their children but for working and even combining jobs and education to get ahead economically. The debates over welfare reform in 1995 and 1996 made the power of public opinion on this topic very clear, as a 60-year-old programme that provided cash benefits to enable poor single mothers to be home with their children was replaced by a programme offering time-limited benefits linked to job training and work requirements. To the public, in other words, the value of family self-sufficiency trumps the value of having a parent as care-giver for the very young—if the family's economic independence is at stake.

ROLE FOR CHILDCARE

The decade of the 1990s marked a crucial transition in public acceptance of the idea that childcare is essential, even for infants and toddlers, if mothers are obliged to work. To help low-income mothers enter the labour force, Sylvester reports, the public is willing to pay for childcare. Indeed, public support has held up during an impressive increase in funding for childcare subsidies for low-income families. Since 1992, combined federal and state subsidy funding has nearly tripled.

In 1999, fully 1.8 million children received childcare subsidies each month, and about one-half million of those children were under age three. As important as it has been to the development of American childcare policy, however, this public support for subsidies does not yet represent a full-blown embrace of childcare, or a commitment to create a system of safe and reliable childcare services.

Research examining children's experiences in childcare underscores the need to address the quality of infant and toddler care. Not only do physical hazards often exist even in licensed childcare settings, but harsh, inattentive, or unresponsive relationships between caregivers and children also threaten children's development. Observers in large-scale, multisite studies of childcare provided in both centre and home settings have found that half the care settings experienced by infants and toddlers are poor or only fair, not good or excellent. No one type of care has proven superior to others for children under age three, however. For example, one study found that children who were six months of age fared best when they were alone with their caregivers. A follow-up study revealed that as toddlers, the children benefited from being in a centre environment with educated teachers and plentiful opportunities to explore.

When the focus is on children under age three, many Americans hesitate to embrace the idea of group care in centres or family childcare homes where the parents do not know the care-givers. So-called "institutional" care is not, according to focus groups and surveys, a desirable option for the very young. Nor do many parents agree with professionals and researchers that training increases the ability of caregivers to offer the love, stimulation, and physical attention that infants and toddlers need.

When children are of age three or four, however, the value of exposure to group experiences, trained teachers, and learning materials is more apparent to parents and policy-makers alike. The statistics on the use of childcare during the first three years of life reported by Phillips and Adams in this chapter parallel these opinions. Of the infants and toddlers whose mothers worked in 1997, 27 per cent were cared for by a relative, 22 per cent in centres, 17 per cent in family childcare homes, and 7 per cent with nannies.

Alarming media stories about inattentive or abusive childcare situations have heightened concerns about the risks of placing babies in non-familial care. Rather than fuelling demand for more government intervention to ensure the safety and quality of childcare settings, however, concerns about childcare have reinforced the American emphasis on the decision-making role of parents. Most childcare subsidies (and the federal childcare tax credit that benefits a wide swath of middle-income American families) can be used to pay for any care that is operating legally, whether it is provided by a next-door neighbour or by a for-profit childcare centre.

The burden of choosing acceptable care is left to the parents, whereas public investments in quality improvements are minimal and regulations are unevenly enforced. In such a laissez-faire policy climate, poor quality care too often is allowed to put children's development at risk. What can be done?

WHO IS RESPONSIBLE?

A variety of Government policies affect care-giving by all families. For instance, tax, employment, and welfare policies oblige parents to work or enable them to remain home; and both regulatory and funding policies shape the market of childcare services where parents shop for non-familial care. As Sylvester notes, however, American values concerning self-sufficiency and childrearing mingle with attitudes toward government to create a narrow social focus on family responsibilities and privacy.

The tradition of American family policy is to assume that "citizens will provide for their own needs through employment; the government steps in only in the event of family breakdown or loss of employment." Indeed, Knitzer in this chapter describes how federal funding for children targets those who are poor, maltreated, and vulnerable.

Knitzer argues that government efforts are focused on supporting the economic role of families, and little attention goes to their care-giving role. By contrast, in most of the European countries described by Waldfogel in this issue, governments use the tools of public policy to advance positive goals for families and children—especially during the first three years of life. Policies seek to encourage childbearing while ensuring that women and men have equal opportunities in education and employment. The public in such countries expects Government and business leaders to provide working conditions, leave and benefit policies, and publicly funded childcare programmes that will help parents balance work and care-giving.

In contrast, when asked directly in public opinion surveys, parents in the United States seldom call for government help in resolving the work-family dilemmas they face. That finding seems surprising. Perhaps, in this country, parents do not want Government authorities to dictate family decisions. Some may fear government scrutiny of their care-giving; others may not want to appear to be unable to manage their responsibilities. Instead, American parents take it upon themselves to find their own, personal solutions to the tensions between the demands of employment and care-giving.

SUPPORTING CHOICE, PROVIDING OPTIONS

A core tenet of the American value system is an emphasis on individual rights, followed quickly by an emphasis on family privacy and integrity, and a preference for market forces over government action. All these values and preferences contribute to a climate in family policy that emphasises choice. In a nation as diverse in cultures and demographics as the United States, it makes sense that successful family policies have built systems that offer a wide array of choices. Hopefully, families will be treated fairly, even as they choose contrasting ways of balancing their work and care-giving responsibilities.

For instance, support for "parent choice" has been a much-touted goal of the last decade's childcare subsidy systems, and now most subsidies are paid through vouchers that do not oblige the recipient to use a predetermined type of care. Previously, public agencies often contracted with specific childcare programmes (usually centres) to serve subsidised children. Like the tax dollars returned to families who deduct childcare expenses from their taxes using the Dependent Care Tax Credit, subsidy vouchers are a flexible form of assistance to parents. Even so, these policies are criticised for not supporting many choices parents would like to make. For example, as Phillips and Adams explain, subsidies vouchers cannot be used to purchase costly childcare options. Conservatives argue that the provision of childcare subsidies discriminates against families in which one parent chooses not to work in order to care for the children. A broader lens could integrate attention to childcare and family policies, including supports for both parental and non-parental care, in the same discussion.

Waldfogel in this chapter highlights the value of policies in other countries that give parents the flexibility to make different care-giving and employment choices. Such policies offer parents equivalent support regardless of what mix of parental care and childcare they use. That article's international comparison underscores the fact that, in the United States, scant public funding exists to support any of the options families use to balance work and care-giving. In the words of one policy analyst, Without paid parental leave, parents of limited means find it difficult to care for an infant (or toddler) at home.

Without having subsidised childcare facilities, parents find it difficult to place a preschool child in a desirable facility. Proclaiming the rights of families to make their own work and care-giving choices is mere rhetoric, unless it is backed up by supports that offer families across the income spectrum viable options for remaining home, securing quality childcare, or combining the two. As Waldfogel notes, "What is best for one child or one family may not be optimal for another child or family," and the choice that works for a child or family at one time may not be suitable a year later.

In fact, no care option is currently extensive, affordable, reliable, or good enough to enable American families at all income levels to feel confident that the right relationships and experiences will surround their vulnerable young children. The articles in this issue highlight three particular policies challenges:

- Few parents have access to paid parental leave, part-time work schedules, and income supports sufficient to allow them to remain home as caregivers for even six months. Low-wage workers who have the fewest options overall are the least likely to enjoy flexible employment with family-friendly benefits.
- Formal, licensed childcare for infants is costly, scarce, and too often of poor quality. Large groups and child-adult ratios, low wages that lead to staff turnover, and lack of training undermine the quality of the relationships between caregivers and children that are the heart and soul of early care-giving.
- Childcare arrangements with relatives, available to some families but not to many others, can be flexible

and trustworthy, or fragile and unsatisfactory. Although public subsidies can now go to pay relative caregivers, few communities have created networks of information and support to strengthen the care these individuals offer to children.

As flawed as they are, these are the major options that families rely on to care for infants and toddlers. Viewing them as a continuum of alternatives that every family may tap at one time or another focuses attention where it should be—on common problems and cross-cutting solutions. Armed with a broad understanding of problems and public priorities, and heartened by concrete experiences, policy-makers and practitioners can start work building new supports for families with babies.

Recommendation: Government policies should assure that all families have supports for childrearing during the first years of life, including leaves for parents who choose to be home and access to good childcare that is safe, affordable, and appropriate to the child and family.

The Family and Medical Leave Act of 1993 (FMLA) gives many employees the right to an unpaid, job-protected 12-week leave to care for a newborn and tend to other family concerns, and the Childcare and Development Fund (CCDF) is the major source of funding for childcare subsidies that low-income families can use to offset the cost of childcare while they work.

In each case, a federal policy action sets in place a framework (a mandate in the case of the FMLA and a block grant to the states in the case of the CCDF) that is implemented and elaborated by state governments and the efforts of private employers and community institutions. For the families covered by these policies, the right to family leave and access to childcare subsidies create better options for both spending time at home and turning outside to arrange childcare.

TIME AT HOME: FAMILY LEAVE

For many families, as for the general public, the most appealing care-giving arrangement for a new baby or a toddler is care by a stay-at-home parent. Parental care offers a baby continuity and security, along with the depth of feeling and attentiveness that accompany the parent-child bond. It gives the parent a chance to participate in the baby's development, rejoicing in each step forward while anticipating the next. It ensures that crucial information about the baby's needs and experiences does not fall through the cracks of communication between parent and caregiver. However, for most American families today, it also means that one parent must stop contributing income to the family budget. Realistically, the question in most households is whether a parent can afford to stay home at all with the new baby.

Since 1993, when the FMLA became law, about one-half of American workers have had a legal right to take 12 weeks of leave to care for a new baby or a foster or adopted child, or to handle an illness in the family—without losing their jobs. The report by Asher and Lenhoff in this chapter describes the political battle to pass the FMLA, outlines the provisions of the law, and highlights its limitations. Popular support for family leave was important in sustaining momentum behind this legislation, and public opinion now strongly favours providing pay during periods of leave.

After the law passed, the non-partisan federal Commission on Leave contracted for surveys of the law's impact on employers and employees to be conducted in 1995 and again in 2000. The findings from these surveys show that, although employers resisted the law's passage and do not support the imposition of such government mandates, most report that complying with the law has not been burdensome (85 per cent in 1995 and 64 per cent in 2000 called compliance easy). Nor has it cut productivity for the great majority (93 per cent in 1995 and 84 per cent in 2000 reported no negative impacts on productivity). The Department of Labour's Website provides the following summary of the survey findings:

> *"The FMLA has succeeded in replacing the piecemeal nature of voluntary employer leave policies and state leave statutes with a consistent and uniform standard. The FMLA has not been the burden to business that some had feared. For most employers, compliance is easy, the costs are non-existent or small, and the effects are minimal. Most periods of leave are short, most employees return to work, and reduced turnover seems to be a tangible positive effect."*

A report on the survey of employees conducted in 2000 shows that 18 per cent of all the leaves taken (short and long) were used by parents to care for a newborn or to welcome a foster or adopted child. A special analysis of leave use by parents with young children indicated that over one-third of the mothers (36 per cent) and one-third of the fathers (34 per cent) who took leave used it for newborn care. Clearly, the existence of job-protected leave helps many families with care-giving during the first life-changing weeks after a birth.

LIMITED ELIGIBILITY FOR LEAVE

As important as it is, however, the FMLA has significant limitations both in its coverage and in the help it provides. As Asher and Lenhoff explain, the law applies only to employers with 50 employees or more. Moreover, within covered worksites, the only employees eligible for leave are those who have worked for the employer for 12 months and 1,250 hours (about 25 hours per week).

Overall, the Department of Labour reports that about two-thirds of the American labour force work for employers (public and private) who are covered by the FMLA, and 55 per cent of all workers (but only 47 per cent of private-sector workers) are eligible for leaves.

Not covered by the law, therefore, are those who are just entering the labour force, employees who have changed jobs, or those who work part-time or on a temporary basis. These workers, along with those at small companies, are also unlikely to be offered leave by their employers on a voluntary basis. In other words, the workers not covered by the FMLA are those who are most likely to need its mandate to secure a leave.

Now that research shows the FMLA's requirements are not damaging to most businesses, it is important to make the guarantee of 12 weeks of leave universal, first by extending the law to cover midsize businesses (those with 25-50 employees, encompassing 13 million more workers), then to include small businesses. Innovative strategies that may not be entirely employer-based will then be needed to provide equivalent protection to part-time, temporary, and recently hired workers.

Recommendation: State and federal governments should provide income to those who take family leave for newborn care through a funding pool that combines public funds with contributions from employers and employees.

UNPAID LEAVE

The second key limitation of the FMLA highlighted in the report by Asher and Lenhoff is the fact that, because the leave guaranteed by law is unpaid, it is of practical value only to those employees who can forego earnings for up to three months.

This limitation is regularly cited as a key reason why only 16 per cent of FMLA-covered employees take leave each year. Overall, one-third of leave-takers received no pay while they were away from their jobs. This may be one reason why 54 per cent of the leaves taken were shorter than 10 days in duration, rather than the 12 weeks guaranteed by the FMLA.

In practice, many employers go beyond the mandates of the law and choose to offer paid leave (which is why no more than one-third go without pay during leave). However, as Friedman in this issue makes clear, voluntary employer benefits provide more advantages to highly-paid workers than they offer to low-wage workers. The 2000 survey of FMLA usage indicates that four of five high-wage workers (80 per cent) who earned over $75,000 per year were paid during their leave.

By contrast, only one of four workers (26 per cent) who earned less than $20,000 per year received any compensation during leave. Clearly, low-income parents facing a strained budget and the added costs of a new baby understand that they cannot afford to avail themselves of the FMLA's unpaid leave. To them, the law is no more than an attractive phrase. To make the guarantees envisioned by the law and its public supporters real to the families who need them the most, a strategy must be devised for paying parents during FMLA-covered leaves.

Recommendation: State and federal governments should extend the protections of the Family and Medical Leave Act to workers in midsized and eventually small businesses.

LEAVING WELFARE FOR EMPLOYMENT

The parents who are least likely to benefit from the FMLA's protections are those who are attempting to move from welfare dependence to work and self-sufficiency, because they are new employees who are likely to receive low wages and no fringe benefits. These families remain, for a time, connected to the welfare system now known as Temporary Assistance for Needy Families, or TANF.

As Knitzer explains, welfare reform changed society's expectation of the poor single mothers who qualify for cash assistance (one-third of whom had a child under age three in 1999). Work requirements now confront welfare recipients even when they have infants less than a year old. Knitzer also points out that welfare rules in twelve states require work by women whose babies are no more than three months old; in four states, work must begin at six months. The other states require work when the child is age one, or later.

The minimal FMLA standard provides three months of leave to families of all income levels, most of whom have some assets and two parents who can share household and care-giving tasks. However, the challenges faced by new mothers on welfare are much steeper, as they single-handedly cope with a new baby and the myriad problems of poverty, while simultaneously seeking to enter the labour market, secure benefits like sick time and paid leave, and find affordable and acceptable childcare arrangements for their babies.

The interests of American taxpayers are best served by helping these mothers succeed by extending more assistance to them for the first year of the child's life as they set up viable ways of handling the pressures of low-wage employment and childcare.

Recommendation: No state should require welfare recipients to work before their babies are six months old. A one-year exemption from work requirements is more appropriate, given the disproportionate difficulties that poor single mothers face in meeting the needs of their babies as they strive toward self-sufficiency.

The extensions and corrections to the FMLA that are recommended here stop well short of providing American working parents the same opportunity to remain home to care for their infants that their counterparts in most industrialised countries enjoy, as Waldfogel explains. Indeed, a recent review of international developments regarding parental leave notes that "worldwide, 128 countries of the 172 responding to the International Social Security Association in 1999 provided at least some paid and job-protected maternity leave."

The international average is now 16 weeks of paid leave. Nonetheless, the changes to American leave policy suggested here are important steps toward establishing a more equitable approach to family leave—one that provides equivalent protections to workers up and down the wage scale. When a universal and fair structure is in place, later reforms can and should extend the duration of paid leave to at least the ten months recommended by Waldfogel, or the one year we recommend for welfare families. By doing so, the nation's leaders can show their esteem for the relationships between babies and their parents that are so crucial to early development.

TURNING TO CHILDCARE: SUBSIDY FUNDING

Even with increased access to family leave, working mothers soon will find themselves searching for childcare, hoping to find caregivers who are warm, reliable, and responsive. Yet, while the nation's youngest children are entering childcare in growing numbers, earlier and earlier in their lives, few would claim that the decentralised childcare market is prepared to offer them the safe, stimulating, nurturing care they deserve.

On the contrary, of all childcare services, care for infants and toddlers is the most scarce, expensive, and disappointing from a quality perspective. Combined with improved leave policies that would give parents more opportunity to care for their babies themselves, improved childcare policies are needed to ensure that the care-giving that takes place outside the family is affordable, trustworthy, and good for babies.

A closer look at the largest governmental investment in childcare, the Childcare and Development Fund (CCDF) that funds childcare subsidies to help low-income families pay for care, suggests that more could be done to protect these most innocent Americans. The growth of childcare subsidy funding during the 1990s has been an important step toward coherent public investment in childcare. As is the case with the FMLA, however, the CCDF has limitations.

If those limitations are addressed, the next generation of childcare investments can further strengthen the childcare options available to parents.

INCREASED ACCESS AND AFFORDABILITY

The most immediate challenge that parents of infants confront, when they start a search for childcare, is that of affordability. Phillips and Adams report in this issue that centre-based care for one infant costs about $6,000 per year, which is more than 14 per cent of the median income of $43,275 for a three-person family in 1999.

The high cost of care hits low-income families even harder. To help them pay for childcare while they work, the CCDF provides federally funded childcare subsidies to low-income families with a child under age 13. To be eligible, families must be working or seeking to leave welfare and can earn no more than 85 per cent of the state's median income.

Parents are assured maximum freedom to choose any childcare provider who meets applicable state standards. Within those broad parameters, states design their subsidy programmes and set more specific eligibility rules, reimbursement rates, and procedures. As Knitzer reports, in 1998 the federal allocation for the CCDF was $3.5 billion in federal funds, to which $1.7 billion in state matching funds was added. Even after significant increases throughout the 1990s, however, the CCDF could help only 12 per cent of the 15 million children estimated to be eligible for federal assistance, leaving many struggling to pay the steep cost of care for children under age three.

Recommendation: Public funding for childcare subsidies should be significantly expanded and sustained, given the reliance of low-income families on maternal earnings and the high cost of infant and toddler childcare.

IMPROVING QUALITY

The CCDF is a funding programme, not a law imposing mandates or requirements like the FMLA, and as currently structured it does little to ensure or upgrade the quality of services available to families. But it could contribute to quality. The studies of childcare mentioned earlier have yielded a simple recipe for quality infant and toddler care.

According to the National Academy of Sciences, young children benefit from care that offers them ample verbal and cognitive stimulation, sensitive and responsive care-giving, and generous amounts of attention and support. These positive experiences are most prevalent when the children are in small groups, when the child-adult ratios are low, and when caregivers are educated, well-compensated, and stable in their roles (turnover among childcare staff averages 30 per cent per year). All these features of good care for infants and toddlers contribute to its cost, however. The CCDF subsidy programme, therefore, can use funding to encourage quality improvements.

For instance, raising the ceilings on allowable payments and using differential rates to recognise care that is demonstrated to be of higher quality are methods of supporting quality. A more flexible approach already built into the CCDF is the requirement that states use 4 per cent of their federal childcare funding for quality improvement.

These funds can support activities to educate consumers about childcare, to expand supply, or to strengthen programmes by providing training, offering stipends to encourage staff retention, or creating toy lending libraries or facility improvement grants.

Establishing a set-aside for quality is an important step, but it will take significantly more than 4 per cent of subsidy funding to have a detectable impact on the quality of the care provided in the sprawling American market of diverse childcare services. One challenge is that the number of child cares programmes keeps growing. The number of childcare centres nationwide expanded by 21 per cent from 1990 to 1997, whereas the number of registered family childcare homes more than doubled.

As noted earlier, subsidy funding nearly tripled over that period. Models exist for linking programme expansion with parallel investments in programme quality, as demonstrated by the reports issued by Fenichel and Mann on Early Head Start, and by Lucas on military childcare. When the dramatic expansion of Head Start began to erode the quality of programmes, federal legislation stipulated that about 25 per cent of funding increases should go to quality improvement. The 4 to 5 million infants and toddlers in childcare deserve no less protection.

Recommendation: The federal Government should significantly increase the percentage of CCDF funds earmarked for quality improvements and link the percentage to future expansions in subsidy funding. State policy-makers should add funding and invest quality dollars based on input from community leaders, advocates, childcare representatives, and parents.

STRENGTHENING ALL TYPES OF CARE

The broad, flexible subsidies provided by the CCDF have given low-income families more access to a variety of types of childcare. To permit parents unfettered choice of childcare providers, states have channelled 85 per cent of the CCDF funding to vouchers that can be used to pay any legal childcare provider identified by the parent (some states also give cash to parents).

Vouchers and cash payments do little to improve the quality of childcare, but they do allow subsidies to flow to the full range of care settings in which infants and toddlers are found, providing resources to caregivers of all types, including relatives and others who may not be licensed.

As explained by Zinsser in this chapter, many families prefer to have relatives care for their infants and toddlers, and indeed 27 per cent of children under age three are cared for by relatives. About one-eighth of the federal CCDF funds went to these caregivers in 1998. The fact that public funds now support this informal, familial type of care has sparked both debate and innovation.

State childcare agencies and childcare professionals are devising creative ways of offering information and support to a continuum of caregivers and childcare settings that stretches from care by parents on the one hand, to care in professional centres on the other.

In this chapter, Zinsser, Fenichel and Mann, Lucas, and Bodenhorn and Kelch describe different approaches to the challenge of supporting and upholding the quality of care provided in different settings. Flexible, creative thinking along these lines can yield pay-offs for parents as they place their trust in America's childcare providers.

Recommendation: Appropriate strategies for overseeing, informing, and supporting the different types of caregivers who work with infants and toddlers should be devised by professionals, supported with public funds, and made available to care-givers of all types—childcare centres, licensed family childcare homes, relatives, and parents.

GOVERNMENT AS A PARTNER TO PARENTS

The alert reader has no doubt noticed that the recommendations throughout this chapter are directed primarily toward policy-makers in federal and state governments. This is not a coincidence. The earlier discussion of public attitudes emphasised the American tradition of assigning only a limited role to government when it comes to family concerns, especially concerns as intimate and important as decisions about care-giving in the first years of life. Sylvester in this issue described the skepticism many Americans have about the ability of "Government Institutions" to help address children's needs for safety, love, and attention.

The image of a faceless, domineering bureaucracy seems the antithesis of the intimate, caring relationships that children need. However, Knitzer offers an alternative image of elected officials and the agencies they lead standing beside parents and community organisations, as partners offering financial assistance and oversight to complement the concrete care-giving efforts of childcare providers and family members.

Most commonly, discussions of the balance between work and care-giving focus not on Government's leaders but on working mothers and their employers. The article by Friedman describes the leading strategies that family-friendly employers have developed to help their employees soften the collision between demands from work and home.

In the booming economy that dominated the 1990s, tight labour markets made recruitment and retention of staff problematic, and work-family programmes and policies gained popularity. In practice, however, family-friendly workplace policies are offered by a small percentage of employers and they target primarily highly-paid staff—the employees whom employers work hardest to recruit and retain. For example, a Harvard business school graduate asked during an interview, "What's your company going to do about my two-year-old daughter?"

The results of such negotiations between parent and employer, of course, reflect the power each one brings to the bargaining table, and so work-family initiatives designed for the manager trained at Harvard seldom trickle down to the ranks of low-wage workers who are easily replaced. Indeed, many low-wage workers get by without even basic employer-provided benefits, such as health care or paid vacation days.

The fact is that businesses are engaged in business, and competitiveness and profits define their success. They will invest in work-family supports, or not, to the extent that doing so enhances productivity or provides a return on investment. That is understandable. It is not the role of business to assure equity throughout society. That role is assigned to Government, our elected leaders.

Therefore, responsibility for ensuring fair access to supports for families must be given to Government with its toolbox of regulations, legal mandates, and funding to pay for tax incentives, subsidies, and service programmes. As one corporate consultant put it, "A family-friendly society is much preferred to a family-friendly corporation." By taking steps to build on the important policies established during the 1990s—the Family and Medical Leave Act and the Childcare and Development Fund—we can move a long way toward creating a society that is more friendly toward infants, toddlers, and their families than the society with which we entered the decade of the 1990s.

There is not time to wait. Each year, almost 4 million children are born and another 4 million pass their third birthdays and move from toddlerhood to the challenges of preschool. Their small hands are reaching up toward their parents and caregivers. As those hard-pressed adults respond to the children's appeals, it is time for the broader society to add another steadying hand. We should give America's infants and toddlers the strongest foundation we can, through support for the caregivers who shelter and raise them.

CHILDCARE SOLUTIONS

Every new parent holding a newborn child, experiences the fundamental and heartfelt desire to nurture this new life. In America in the 1990s, providing for this child often means finding a supportive childcare environment. Out-of-home childcare is an increasingly important facet of everyday life. Not only are more children entering childcare facilities, but these children are entering at an earlier age. A substantial proportion of children begin out-of-home care as early as 10 weeks of age. Further, changes in social assistance policy and the topography of the American workforce will increase the need for access to affordable and safe childcare. Society is just beginning to respond to this significant change in early childhood.

Along with the increased requirements for quality facilities comes an increasingly complex set of demands placed on childcare providers. These include the need to provide a developmentally stimulating and creative environment for all children, including those with acute or chronic medical needs. At the same time, childcare professionals are now often asked to assist parents in managing the increasingly complex world of childrearing. These are, by and large, new issues in this country. Looking outside our boundaries to see how other nations have found childcare solutions may provide some direction. However, as with most sociologically driven issues such as healthcare restructuring, Americans will require solutions that fit our national temperament and economic perspective.

This issue of *The Pfizer Journal* emerged from a daylong meeting of a remarkable panel of paediatricians and experts in childcare, which was sponsored by Pfizer. Pfizer convened this National Panel on Childcare and Health because of its interest in this topic both as a healthcare company and as a Fortune 100 employers with over 46,000 employees worldwide, many of whom are affected by these issues.

The new extended family framework of today's childcare environment not only presents increased challenges but also new opportunities for caring and nurturing. One of the principal issues that the Panel focused on is the myriad of opportunities to view childcare centres as places to deliver health and wellness information and education.

There is an ever-increasing number of innovative programmes that have begun to do this. These include programmes such as Smart Start in North Carolina, which stresses preventive and early health intervention services, as well as the federal Head Start programmes, which have—among other accomplishments—increased compliance with childhood vaccination regimens. Another programme is the Back to Sleep programme led by the National Institute of Child Health and Human Development, and the American Academy of Pediatrics, which has had a dramatic impact in reducing the occurrence of sudden infant death syndrome.

These landmark programmes are being developed further and being showcased to demonstrate how the needs of a broader range of communities and children can be met. The National Panel on Childcare and Health identified seven areas where childcare providers, policy-makers, employers, and others can focus attention as advocates for children.

Pfizer is proud to demonstrate its commitment to children's health. Two such initiatives, which Pfizer supports:

- *Bright Futures*, a jointly sponsored programme by the Maternal and Child Health Bureau of the Health Resources and Services Administration and the Medicaid Bureau of the Health Care Financing Administration, which provides guidelines for health supervision of infants, children and adolescents. The programme is designed to enhance the way health professionals practise as well as the way families view preventive care, increase family participation in childcare, and foster partnerships between families, health professionals and communities.
- *Eagle's Circle*, a unique demonstration project of exercise and fitness created by Pfizer's Pediatric Team and James Sgritto, a certified exercise physiologist and a manager on that team. This programme offers a regimen of exercise, health education and peer-group discussion to help children with asthma understand their disease and develop positive

behaviours. Pilot projects are under way in New York City, Memphis, and New Orleans.

The physical environment can either contribute to children's development and support staff and parent goals or create a permanent impediment to the operation of a high quality programme. Designing a high-quality, developmentally appropriate childcare facility is a highly complex task which requires specialised and unique skills. The design and layout of the physical environment, which includes the building, interior finishes, outdoor spaces, selection of equipment and room arrangement has a profound impact on children's learning and behaviour and on teachers' abilities to efficiently do their jobs.

Children need age-appropriate physical environments that support and promote child-directed and child-initiated play. The environment must promote and positively support the child's interaction with space, materials and people. Teachers and caregivers also need highly functional, easy-to-use environments. When the environment supports both and is working for children and adults, it is easier for adults to focus on facilitating each child's play and learning.

Facilities that fail to support a high-quality programme are usually the result of well-meaning intentions gone awry. The problem can usually be traced to both the expertise of the design participants and the design process. The product can only be as good as the process that creates it and the expertise of the design participants.

The first problem is that architects and designers who understand the principles of design often have little knowledge of child development and the operation of childcare centres. Many times architects and designers create and choose designs that look good to them but may not be functional and practical in a childcare centre. Some buildings end up being architectural monuments that are over-designed with too much of the money being spent on the outside facade.

The more money that is being spent on the exterior shell of the building, the less money there will be for inside functional details like high quality finishes, appropriate furniture and equipment, adequate numbers of sinks and interior windows/doors—all details which can better support children and staff needs. Another limitation of architects is that they often do not understand that children just cannot adapt to inappropriate design like adults.

Although there are anthropometric charts to assist them in making design elements the appropriate heights and depths, architects fail to understand, for example, that a toddler sink which is too high is unusable and one that is too low is unsafe since the children will climb inside. Children cannot adapt to design errors in height or depth. It simply must be age-appropriate the first time to work successfully.

The second problem that contributes to poor design is that the directors and teachers who know children and understand their needs rarely know how to translate their teaching and administrative skills to the design of space and the language used by architects and designers. Most childcare practitioners may not be able to offer the best design solutions because they do not have a broad enough experience base.

Due to being hampered by their existing paradigms, practitioners may be unaware of many solutions or may not be able to understand the downside of a particular solution. It is truly difficult to think of things you have never seen or read about. Add to the problem that practitioners do not speak the same language as architects and designers, and you will see why the multitude of details which can produce a high-quality, developmentally-appropriate facility fall through the cracks.

The third problem that contributes to poor design has to do with the design process itself. The traditional design process is sequential like a relay race. The architect grabs the baton from the client, does the site and floor plan and passes the baton to the structural engineer. The structural engineer finishes their job and starts the baton on its path to a long line of specialists who, one by one, create the lighting, electrical and mechanical systems and interior design. Then the baton is passed to the staff to select and lay out the equipment. By then so many constraints have often been created by the architectural design that a quality equipment layout becomes impossible.

One of the big problems with this sequential relay approach is that each stage of design squeezes the stage after it, often closing off options that could have improved quality, reduced costs and sped up construction. Another problem is that each person has a vision only of his or her brief segment of the race; there is no unified vision to guide the design. Instead of a team working together to create a high quality, developmentally appropriate facility, the individuals do the best they can with what's been handed to them. They lose the benefits of a broad view and collaborative creativity.

Designing a children's facility this way makes as much sense as, in the words of physicist David Bohm, gluing together the fragments of a broken mirror to see a true reflection. By the time the picture begins to come together, it may be too late to change decisions made at the first leg of the race without costing too much time or money. Once the details have been entered on construction documents, any subsequent necessary changes will entail change orders costs, confusing details and possible construction delays.

The problem of this traditional approach is especially true with the design of children's facilities. By the time the owner is passed the baton, many design decisions, such as the floor plan, type of construction and finishes, have already been made. Often, the facility's very design is creating an unfriendly child and adult environment, but the flexibility to correct the underlying design problems has been lost.

Our company believes that high quality, developmentally appropriate facilities are created through what is called concurrent design. Concurrent design means pulling together all the experts who design the facility and those who operate it at the same time. Everyone jumps into the sandbox at once, with specialists from many different areas participating as members of a multi-disciplinary, cross-functional design team from the beginning.

Programme goals, curriculum, children's needs, staff needs and parents' needs drive the concurrent design process. Other issues that need to be examined at the front end of the process are furniture and equipment and developmental and operating costs prior to designing the physical space. Everything impacts everything.

Function is examined in the process prior to looking at form. For example, many programmes such as Head Start encourage parents to work in the classroom. Parent participation may necessitate more classroom square footage than state licensing standards require. State licensing requirements are only minimums and not necessarily quality standards.

Outdoor areas designed for the inner city may have different durability and vandalism issues than an outdoor area in a rural area. Another example is that some cultural considerations will influence the design process. In a children's facility we designed for Muslims, the parents had mixed feelings about the use of outdoor sand boxes and conceded that they would not wish their children to use it unless it was sanitised regularly.

Several cultures that we have worked with were concerned about privacy issues in the toddler changing table area. Families whom we worked with in South America seemed uncomfortable with large group areas. In order to be culturally sensitive, we adapt our design ideas accordingly. Cultural sensitivity and cultural competency is integral to good design.

The design team needs to be structured and sensitive to staff, parental and community input. The team should have members with specialised expertise in: childcare, early childhood education, Head Start, Early Head Start, child development, children's play design, children's environmental design, infant/toddler care, architecture, landscape architecture, interior design, nature-based outdoor play space design, value engineering, acoustics for children, participatory design, start-up and operating budgets, equipment selection, cultural competency, universal design for children with disabilities and management of early childhood or Head Start centres.

Whether you are working on a renovation or planning a new facility, the design process has a number of steps which are important for the practitioner to understand. The first step will be a preliminary site visit to meet with key staff, parents and sometimes children.

From this meeting will evolve the design requirements such as the age and number of children, group sizes, staffing, curriculum goals, range of activities, designated spaces, square footage requirements, necessary regulations/standards and areas for aesthetics. At the time of the site visit, an inventory will be compiled and photographs taken of the site, existing structures, location of trees, identification of existing plant material, location of the sun, site drainage, and the condition of the building mechanicals and existing mechanical and electrical systems, if appropriate.

The second step in the process is to create a conceptual design to find out what will work best for your programme and to create an overall concept of the building or space. If this stage includes drawings for owner reaction, they will most likely be what are called bubble diagrams to work out adjacency and size issues with no detail. The next step is schematic design which will include a drawing that creates building specifics, relationships, basic furniture layouts, floor plans, mechanical and structural elements.

The last step in the process is the development of the construction drawings and specifications and final selection of all furniture and equipment. These final construction documents are the specific plans which are used to obtain construction bids and permits and the general contractor will use to construct the building. Once construction or renovation begins, it is difficult and expensive to make changes. The set of prints and specifications that you have received contain many details which you will not need to understand; but more importantly they contain a myriad of details that must be executed properly for a high-quality facility, such as sink heights, toilet heights, door locations, sink depth, floor surfaces, window coverings, lighting and acoustics to name a few.

All of these details were developed to best support the use of the space by children, staff and parents. Changes should not be made to these documents or the furniture and equipment without first discussing the ramifications of design changes for children and staff with the design team. An appropriate, high-quality building plan, specifications and furniture and equipment selection will be of little use, if the facility is not built accordingly.

Designing and creating a high quality childcare facility is a complex and lengthy process. By understanding the multi-faceted issues and complexities of designing children's environments, you can better select and work with a qualified design firm that can deliver the high quality, comprehensive and integrated design solutions that are required for a childcare facility to meet staff's, parents', community's and children's needs.

TYPES OF CHILDCARE

Need a little extra help choosing the right childcarer? Whether it's a childminder or a nanny you're looking for, here you can read a quick guide to the different types of childcare available to you.

Nannies: Nannies look after your children in the family home, usually while you are working. They can provide high quality, flexible childcare in the familiar surroundings of the family home. They can look after children of any age and should provide plenty of fun and learning opportunities in a safe environment. Nannies can often work flexible hours and can be a suitable option, if you work at times when other forms of childcare are not available.

Not all nannies are trained and there are no legal requirements for a person applying for a job as a nanny. Types of nanny you may come across include:

- *Live-in nannies:* This type of nanny lives with the family they are working for, who provides them with food and a private bedroom in addition to their salary.
- *Daily nannies:* This type of nanny comes to the family home each day. Baby-sitting in the evenings might be arranged as part of the terms of employment, or in exchange for extra pay.
- *Nanny-share:* An arrangement whereby a nanny is shared by two families. If a nanny is shared by more than two families, they may be required to register as a childminder.

Mother's Helps: Mother's help usually work alongside you, helping with childcare and general household work. Mother's helps are unlikely to have formal childcare qualifications, but may be experienced.

Maternity Nurses: These are specially trained to take care of new babies for upto three months after the birth. They generally live with the family.

Au Pairs: These are single young people, who come from a member state of the European Community or one of a limited number of other countries. They come to the UK to study English and, while staying with families, help in the home for a maximum of five hours a day. They must have at least two full days off each week, and be provided with meals, an allowance and their own room. Au pairs are not usually trained to work with children and therefore, are not generally considered as being suited to looking after pre-school children while you are at work. However, they can be a good option for providing after-school childcare.

Childminders: A childminder is a professional childcarer who provides safe, good quality care on domestic premises, usually the childminder's own home. To look after children under the age of eight they must be registered with, and be inspected by, the Office for Standards in Education (Ofsted). Although Ofsted will expect childminders to meet required standards of care, it is up to you as the parent(s) to negotiate with them the exact terms and conditions of their employment.

Home Childcarers: A home childcarer is a person who looks after children within the parents' home. They are professional childcarers, offering children safe, good quality care and providing them with play and learning opportunities that contribute to their development. Home childcarers have to meet criteria set in a Code of Practice that is monitored by Ofsted.

The Home Childcarers Scheme was set up in April 2003 to help widen the availability of tax credit support by ensuring that parents can access approved forms of childcare to use within their own homes. At present, only registered childminders can apply to be approved by Ofsted as home childcarers. Since the Government has announced an extension to this scheme, the Sure Start Unit in the Department for Education and Skills are preparing a consultation on who should carry out the work and how the approval and registration process should operate in future.

❑

2

CHILD GROWTH

Child Development, physical, intellectual, social, and emotional changes that occur from birth to adolescence. Although people change throughout their lives, developmental changes are especially dramatic in childhood.

During this period, a dependent, vulnerable newborn grows into a capable young person who has mastered language, is self-aware, can think and reason with sophistication, has a distinctive personality, and socialises effortlessly with others. Many abilities and characteristics developed in childhood last a lifetime.

Some developments in behaviour and thought are very similar for all children. Around the world, most infants begin to focus their eyes, sit up, and learn to walk at comparable ages, and children begin to acquire language and develop logical reasoning skills at approximately the same time. These aspects of individual growth are highly predictable.

Other aspects of development show a much wider range of individual differences. Whether a child becomes outgoing or shy, intellectually advanced or average, or energetic or subdued depends on many unique influences whose effects are difficult to predict at the child's birth.

A variety of factors influence child development. Heredity guides every aspect of physical, cognitive, social, emotional, and personality development.

Family members, peer groups, the school environment, and the community influence how children think, socialise, and become self-aware. Biological factors such as nutrition, medical care, and environmental hazards in the air and water affect the growth of the body and mind.

Economic and political institutions, the media, and cultural values all guide how children live their lives. Critical life events, such as a family crisis or a national emergency, can alter the growth of personality and identity. Most important of all, children contribute significantly to their own development.

This occurs as they strive to understand their experiences, respond in individual ways to the people around them, and choose activities, friends, and interests. Thus, the factors that guide development arise from both outside and within the person.

Why is the study of child development important? One reason is that it provides practical guidance for parents, teachers, childcare providers, and others who care for children. A second reason is that it enables society to support healthy growth. Understanding early brain development, for example, means that parents can provide better opportunities for intellectual stimulation, and society can reduce or eliminate obstacles to healthy brain growth.

Third, the study of child development helps therapists and educators better assist children with special needs, such as those with emotional or learning difficulties. Finally, understanding child development contributes to self-understanding.

We know ourselves better by recognising the influences that have made us into the people we are today.

EARLY VIEWS ON CHILDREN

People have thought very differently about children in different historical eras. In ancient Rome and throughout the Middle Ages, for example, childhood was brief: A boy or girl was considered an "infant" until the age of six, but soon afterward worked alongside adults in the fields, workshop, or home. Children were thought to be born in a state of sin and were viewed as the property of their fathers. Such beliefs contributed to strict discipline of children and neglect of their special needs.

These harsh attitudes softened during the Renaissance and enlightenment as the humanistic spirit of the times caused a rediscovery of the special qualities of childhood. In paintings, for example, young children were depicted more realistically as they played, nursed, and did other childish things, rather than being shown as miniature adults.

The importance of childhood as a unique period of development was understood more fully in the 17th and 18th centuries, as reflected in the writings of two important European thinkers. The English philosopher John Locke argued that the newborn infant comes into the world with no inherited predispositions, but rather with a mind as a tabula rasa (Latin for "blank slate") that is gradually filled with ideas, concepts, and knowledge from experiences in the world. He concluded that the quality of early experiences, particularly how children are raised and educated, shapes the direction of a child's life.

Later, the French philosopher Jean Jacques Rousseau claimed that children at birth are innately good, not evil, and that their natural tendencies should be protected against the corrupting influences of society. The sympathetic, romantic attitude toward children inspired by Rousseau had an important influence on society. For example, the novelists Charles Dickens and Victor Hugo described the exploitation of child labour and highlighted the need for educational and social reform.

SCIENTIFIC STUDY

In the late 19th century, interest in the characteristics and needs of children produced more systematic efforts to study their development. The modern theory of evolution, conceived by British naturalist Charles Darwin, contributed to this interest by arguing that human behaviour is best understood through knowledge of its origins—in both the evolution of the species and the early development of individuals. Darwin himself studied children's growth by writing one of the first "baby biographies," consisting of careful observations of his children.

In the early 1900s, the theory of psychoanalysis focused on the importance of early childhood experiences. American psychologist G. Stanley Hall at Clark University began large-scale investigations of child development through surveys and interviews with the adults who cared for them. For the first time, children warranted scientific attention because of society's interest in their development and well-being.

In the 1920s developmental scientists at other American universities began large-scale observational studies of children and their families, including the Berkeley Growth Studies at the University of California, the Fels Growth Study at Antioch College, and the Harvard Growth Studies at Harvard University. Each investigation studied a large number of children repeatedly over many years to identify changes and consistencies in their behaviour and thinking.

At Stanford University, psychologist Lewis Terman created the Stanford-Binet Intelligence Scale, which remains one of the most widely used assessments of children's intellectual capabilities. Terman also started his own long-term study of highly intelligent children. At Yale University, psychologist Arnold Gesell established a research institute devoted to identifying age norms for a wide variety of behaviours and characteristics. While Gesell believed in the importance of maturation on children's development, other psychologists emphasised the role of learning from environmental influences.

One of these, John B. Watson of Johns Hopkins University, advised parents to treat their offspring in an objective, consistent manner to encourage the development of desired characteristics. Watson believed that all human behaviours could be explained as learned responses to stimuli in the environment, an approach known as behaviourism. This approach to the study of child development remained dominant for the first half of the 20th century.

Although behaviourists contributed much to the study of children, their concepts eventually were viewed as being overly narrow. In the early 1960s scholars began to focus more attention on the work of Swiss psychologist Jean Piaget, who had been studying children's cognitive development since the 1920s. Piaget claimed that children construct new knowledge by applying their current knowledge structures to new experiences and modifying them accordingly. His perspective, called constructivism, emphasised the active role children play in their own mental growth as inquisitive thinkers.

Piaget's theories led to other approaches to the study of child development. In the 1960s and 1970s British psychologist John Bowlby and American psychologist Mary Ainsworth introduced the concept of attachment. They proposed that infants and young children form emotional bonds to their care-givers because, throughout human evolutionary history, close attachments to adults promoted the survival of defenceless children.

In the 1970s and 1980s American psychologist Urie Bronfenbrenner sought to describe child development in terms of ecological and cultural forces. In his model, environmental influences on the child extend well beyond the family and peer group, and include schools and other community agencies, social institutions such as the media, political and economic conditions, and national customs. Other developmental scientists have studied how cultural values guide the skills and attitudes that children acquire as they mature, and how brain maturation influences the development of thinking and feeling.

NATURE AND NURTURE

Scholars have long debated the relative importance of nature (hereditary influences) and nurture (environmental influences) in child development. It was once assumed that these forces operated independently of each other. Today developmental scientists recognise that both influences are essential and are mutually influential. For example, how a child responds to parenting—an environmental influence—is partly determined by the child's temperament and other inherited characteristics.

Likewise, the environment influences how hereditary characteristics develop and are expressed. During the past century, for example, there have been significant increases in average height because of improved nutrition and medical care, even though individual differences in height are strongly influenced by heredity. The conclusion that strongly inherited characteristics are changeable has important practical implications. For instance, even though many features of personality are based on inherited temperament, the family environment is an important influence on a child's personality development. Thus, even a child with a difficult temperament can develop positively in a warm and caring family environment.

Continuity or Stages: Does childhood growth occur continuously and gradually, or is it instead a series of distinct stages? People often think of childhood as a sequence of age-related stages (such as infancy, early childhood, and middle childhood), and many developmental theories portray childhood growth in this manner. Such a view recognises that each period of growth has its own distinct changes, challenges, and characteristics. But many aspects of childhood development are more gradual and continuous, such as the development of physical skills, social abilities, and emotional understanding. Even some milestones that seem to denote a new stage of growth—such as a child's first word—are actually the outcome of a more gradual developmental process.

Stability and Change: Are a person's characteristics primarily shaped by early influences, remaining relatively stable thereafter throughout life? Or does change occur continuously throughout life? Many people believe that early experiences are formative, providing a strong or weak foundation for later psychological growth. This view is expressed in the popular saying "As the twig is bent, so grows the tree." From this perspective, it is crucial to ensure that young children have a good start in life. But many developmental scientists believe that later experiences can modify or even reverse early influences; studies show that even when early experiences are traumatic or abusive, considerable recovery can occur. From this vantage point, early experiences influence, but rarely determine, later characteristics.

Like other basic questions about development, whether early experiences are a determining force or fading influence has practical implications. For example, belief in the importance of early experiences is the basis of efforts to strengthen early childhood education programmes, especially for children from disadvantaged backgrounds, to reduce later difficulties in school achievement.

THEORIES OF CHILD DEVELOPMENT

A theory is an organised set of principles that is designed to explain and predict something. Over the years, psychologists and other scientists have devised a variety of theories with which to explain observations and discoveries about child development. In addition to providing a broader framework of understanding, a good theory permits educated guesses—or hypotheses—about aspects of development that are not yet clearly understood.

These hypotheses provide the basis for further research. A theory also has practical value. When a parent, educator, therapist, or policymaker makes decisions that affect the lives of children, a well-founded theory can guide them in responsible ways.

Theories can also limit understanding, such as when a poor theory misleadingly emphasises unimportant influences on development and underestimates the significance of other factors. It is, therefore, essential that theories are carefully evaluated and tested through research, whose results often lead to improvements in theoretical claims. In addition, when theories are compared and contrasted, their strengths and limitations can be more easily identified.

There are four primary theories of child development: psychoanalytic, learning, cognitive, and socio-cultural. Each offers insights into the forces guiding childhood growth. Each also has limitations, which is why many developmental scientists use more than one theory to guide their thinking about the growth of children.

Psychoanalytic Theories: At the end of the 19th century, Austrian physician Sigmund Freud developed the theory and techniques of psychoanalysis; it formed the basis for several later psychoanalytic theories of human development. Psychoanalytic theories share an emphasis on personality development and early childhood experiences. In the psychoanalytic view, early experiences shape one's personality for an entire lifetime, and psychological problems in adulthood may have their origins in difficult or traumatic childhood experiences.

In addition, psychoanalytic theories emphasise the role of unconscious, instinctual drives in personality development. Some of these drives are sexual or aggressive in quality, and their unacceptability to the conscious mind causes them to be repressed in the unconscious mind. Here, they continue to exert a powerful influence on an individual's behaviour, often without his or her awareness.

Most psychoanalytic theories portray development as a series of stages through which all children proceed. According to Freud, child development consists of five psychosexual stages in which a particular body region is the focus of sensual satisfactions; the focus of pleasure shifts as children progress through the stages.

During the oral stage, from birth to age 1, the mouth, tongue, and gums are the focus of sensual pleasure, and the baby develops an emotional attachment to the person providing these satisfactions (primarily through feeding). During the *anal stage*, from ages 1 to 3, children focus on pleasures associated with control and self-control, primarily with respect to defecation and toilet training. In the *phallic stage*, from ages 3 to 6, children derive pleasure from genital stimulation. They are also interested in the physical differences between the sexes and identify with their same-sex parent. The *latency phase*, from ages 7 to 11, is when sensual motives subside and psychological energy is channelled into conventional activities, such as schoolwork. Finally, during the *genital stage*, from adolescence through adulthood, individuals develop mature sexual interests.

An American psychoanalyst, Erik Erikson proposed a related series of *psychosocial stages* of personality growth that more strongly emphasise social influences within the family. Erikson's eight stages span the entire life course, and, contrary to Freud's stages, each involves a conflict in the social world with two possible outcomes. In infancy, for example, the conflict is "trust vs. mistrust" based on whether the baby is confident that others will provide nurturance and care. In adolescence, "identity vs. role confusion" defines the teenager's search for self-understanding. Erikson's theory thus emphasises the interaction of internal psychological growth and the support of the social world.

Psychoanalytic theories offer a rich portrayal of personality growth that emphasises the complex emotional—and sometimes irrational—forces within each person. These theories are hard to prove or disprove, however, because they are based on unconscious processes inaccessible to scientific experimentation.

Learning Theories: Learning theorists emphasise the role of environmental influences in shaping the way a person develops. In their view, child development is guided by both deliberate and unintended learning experiences in the home, peer group, school, and community. Therefore, childhood growth is significantly shaped by the efforts of parents, teachers, and others to socialise children in desirable ways. According to learning theories, the same principles that explain how people can use a bicycle or computer also explain how children acquire social skills, emotional self-control, reasoning strategies, and the physical skills of walking and running.

One kind of learning occurs when a child's actions are followed by a reward or punishment. A reward, also called a reinforcer, increases the probability that behaviour will be repeated. For example, a young child may regularly draw pictures because she receives praise from her parents after completing each one. A punishment decreases the probability that behaviour will be repeated. For example, a child who touches a hot stove and burns his fingertips is not likely to touch the stove again. American psychologist B. F. Skinner devoted his career to explaining how human behaviour is affected by its consequences—a process he called operant conditioning–and to describing the positive and constructive ways that reinforcement and punishment can be used to guide children's behaviour.

Another kind of learning, classical conditioning, occurs when a person makes a mental association between two events or stimuli. When conditioning has occurred, merely encountering the first stimulus produces a response once associated only with the second stimulus. For example, babies begin sucking when they are put in a familiar nursing posture, children fear dogs whose barking has startled them in the past, and students cringe at the sound of school bells that signal that they are tardy. Classical conditioning was first studied by Russian physiologist Ivan Pavlov in the early 1900s and later by American psychologist John B. Watson.

A third kind of learning consists of imitating the behaviour of others. A boy may acquire his father's style of talking, his mother's tendency to roll her eyes, and his favourite basketball player's moves on the court. In doing so, he also acquires expectations about the consequences of these behaviours. This type of learning has been studied extensively by American psychologist Albert Bandura. His social learning theory emphasises how learning through observation and imitation affects behaviour and thought.

Learning theories provide extremely useful ways of understanding how developmental changes in behaviour and thinking occur and, for some children, why behaviour problems arise. These theories can be studied scientifically and practically applied. Critics point out, however, that because of their emphasis on the guidance of the social environment, learning theorists sometimes neglect children's active role in their own understanding and development.

Cognitive Theories: Understanding how children think is crucial to understanding their development because children's perceptions of life events often determine how these events affect them. For example, a five-year-old who believes that her parents' marital problems are her fault is affected much differently than an adolescent who has a better understanding of marriage and relationships. Cognitive theorists focus on the development of thinking and reasoning as the key to understanding childhood growth.

The best-known theory of cognitive development was developed by Swiss psychologist Jean Piaget, who became interested in how children think and construct their own knowledge. Based on his studies and observations, Piaget theorised that children proceed through four distinct stages of cognitive development: *the sensorimotor stage, the pre-operational stage, the concrete-operational stage, and the formal-operational stage.*

During the *sensorimotor stage*, which lasts from birth to about age 2, understanding is based on immediate sensory experience and actions. Thought is very practical but lacking in mental concepts or ideas. In the pre-operational stage, which spans the pre-school years (about ages 2 to 6), children's understanding becomes more conceptual. Thinking involves mental concepts that are independent of immediate experience, and language enables children to think about unseen events, such as thoughts and feelings. The young child's reasoning is intuitive and subjective. During the *concrete-operational stage*, from about 7 to 11 years of age, children engage in objective, logical mental processes that make them more careful, systematic thinkers. Around age 12 children attain the *formal-operational stage*, when they can think about abstract ideas, such as ethics and justice. They can also reason about hypothetical possibilities and deduce new concepts.

According to Piaget, children progress through these four stages by applying their current thinking processes to new experiences; gradually, they modify these processes to better accommodate reality. This occurs not through direct instruction, but rather through the child's own mental activity and internal motivation to understand.

Information-processing Theory: This theory is based on similarities between the human mind and a computer, both of which are high-speed information-processing devices. These theories describe cognitive growth as the gradual acquisition of more sophisticated strategies for organising information, solving problems, storing and retrieving knowledge, and evaluating solutions. Like Piaget, information-processing theorists believe that children acquire these skills through their everyday efforts to understand and master intellectual challenges.

Cognitive theories provide insights into how a child's mental processes underlie many aspects of his or her development. However, critics argue that Piaget underestimated the sophistication of the cognitive abilities of young children. Information-processing theorists have also been faulted for portraying children as little computers rather than as inventive, creative thinkers.

Socio-cultural Theory: Many developmental scientists believe that children do not proceed through universal stages or processes of development. To socio-cultural theorists, children's growth is deeply guided by the values, goals, and expectations of their culture. In this perspective, children acquire skills valued by their culture—such as reading, managing crops, or using an abacus—through the guidance and support of older people. Thus, developmental abilities may differ for children in different societies, and development cannot be separated from its cultural context.

One of the pioneers of socio-cultural theory was Russian psychologist Lev Vygotsky, whose writings in the 1920s and 1930s emphasised how children's interaction with adults contributes to the development of skills. According to Vygotsky, sensitive adults are aware of a child's readiness for new challenges, and they structure appropriate activities to help the child develop new skills. Adults act as mentors and teachers, leading the child into the *zone of proximal development*—Vygotsky's term for the range of skills that the child cannot perform unaided but can master with adult assistance. A parent may encourage simple number concepts, for example, by counting beads with the child or measuring cooking ingredients together, filling in the numbers that the child cannot remember. As children participate in such experiences daily with parents, teachers, and others, they gradually learn the culture's practices, skills, and values.

Socio-cultural theory highlights how children incorporate culture into their reasoning, social interaction, and self-understanding. It also explains why children growing up in different societies are likely to have significantly different skills. Theorists like Vygotsky are sometimes criticised, however, for neglecting the influence of biological maturation, which guides childhood growth independently of culture.

RESEARCH APPROACHES

Studying children presents many challenges. Young children cannot easily put their understanding into words, and their attention span is limited, so scientists must find creative ways of discovering what they know. In addition, all human development involves change, so scientists must study how behaviour and thinking change over time to derive conclusions about childhood growth.

Developmental scientists often study children in their everyday settings—at home, at school, on the playground, in a childcare centre, or in the neighbourhood—because they seek to understand children's behaviour in these natural contexts. Furthermore, children act more typically in these settings. For some research questions, however, the controlled environment of a laboratory is required—particularly when children's responses to experimental procedures must be carefully studied. Sometimes laboratories are designed to resemble a living room at home so that children feel more comfortable and respond more typically.

There are many methods researchers use to learn about how children act and think. They can simply observe children without intruding on their actions. They can interview children face-to-face or use questionnaires to survey older children about their thoughts, knowledge, and reactions. Researchers may also learn about children by collecting information from others who know them well, such as their parents.

These secondary source reports can be quite informative when children are too young to give reliable information about themselves. Sometimes scientists administer psychological tests—such as tests of intelligence or memory ability—to evaluate what children can do. On occasion, researchers conduct case studies of specific individuals, usually children who have unusual characteristics or exceptional experiences, in the hope of generalising their findings to a larger population.

Experiments are carefully designed procedures, usually conducted in a laboratory setting, that measure children's reactions to specific events. Because their conditions are so carefully controlled, experiments are well suited to understanding the causes of behaviour and development. The experimenter manipulates one factor in a situation, keeping all other variables constant, to determine the effect of that manipulation.

An experiment could be designed, for example, to study how the facial expressions of mothers influence their infants when an unfamiliar adult suddenly appears. In one experimental condition, the mother might be instructed to look cheerful, and in another condition she might be instructed to look frightened. By observing the infant's reaction to the stranger in each condition, and keeping all other aspects of the situation the same, the experimenter could determine the effect of the mother's facial expression.

Collection of physiological data is common in many experiments. For example, experimenters may measure heart rate to determine whether children are excited or emotionally aroused, monitor the brain waves of infants to detect changes in mental state, or track the eye movements of babies to determine exactly how long they gaze at particular objects.

To learn about how children change over time, scientists use one of two basic research designs: longitudinal research and cross-sectional research. In longitudinal research, the same children are repeatedly observed and tested as they are, enabling researchers to identify the later consequences of early influences on them. However, such studies take years to complete, are expensive, and run the risk that the subjects (or researchers) will die, drop out of the study, or become unavailable. In cross-sectional research, different groups of children are observed at each of several ages. This enables scientists to study development more quickly and easily, but the long-term effects of early influences cannot be identified because each child is studied at only one point in time.

In conducting research, developmental scientists must take care to ensure that their studies are objectively designed with procedures that children can understand, and that children are free from stress or coercion when they participate. Considerable thought and creativity are required to balance the needs and perspectives of children with the goals of the scientific study.

PRENATAL DEVELOPMENT AND BIRTH

Human development begins with conception, the fertilisation of an egg by a sperm. Over the next nine months, astounding advances in physical growth occur. The fertilised egg becomes a complex newborn capable of surviving (with assistance) outside of the womb. The prenatal months are not only a time of dramatic developmental changes, but also the most hazardous period of the life course. A developing being is the most vulnerable to harm during periods of very rapid growth. However, hazards to prenatal development can be reduced through the mother's conscientious care of herself and her developing child.

Stages of Prenatal Growth: The nine months of prenatal development are usually divided into three stages. These are the germinal period, the embryonic period, and the fetal period.

During the germinal period, which lasts from conception until day 14, the fertilised egg, called a zygote, undergoes rapid cell division and growth. At the same time, its cells begin to differentiate and cluster to assume specialised roles. For example, some cells begin to form the support structures of the placenta, which will provide food and oxygen to the fetus, while others begin to form structures of the developing human. Another significant achievement of the germinal stage is implantation of the cell mass, now called the blastocyst, into the inner wall of the mother's uterus, where it will remain for the duration of prenatal development. Implantation also triggers hormonal changes in the mother's body that enables it to nurture the developing human.

The embryonic period lasts from day 14 through the eighth week. During this time, major structures and organ systems begin to form. During the fourth week, for example, the brain begins to develop, a primitive heart starts to beat, and the eyes, ears, and mouth begin to form. By eight weeks after conception, the embryo has most of its basic organ systems, facial features have formed, and even fingers and toes have appeared.

During the fetal period, from the ninth week until birth, major organs grow in size and complexity, the muscular and nervous systems develop, and the sex organs form. By the fourth or fifth month, mothers can begin to feel the fetus moving within them. The fetus startles in response to sudden, loud noises outside the womb, and its hiccupping can be detected. Brain development is dramatic. Nearly all nerve cells that the brain will use throughout life are formed, and brain regions become specialised in function. As birth approaches, the fetus grows significantly in size and adds protective fat stores in preparation for life outside the womb.

Hazards to Prenatal Development: Although the mother's protective womb and the structures of the placenta provide considerable protection to the developing human organism, there are many potential hazards to prenatal growth. These hazards can have a devastating impact on the embryo or fetus, especially in the early months of development, when organ systems and body structures are the most unstable and vulnerable. Substances that can harm the embryo or fetus and cause birth defects or death are called teratogens (pronounced ter-AT-oh-jins).

Two factors are important in determining the impact that a particular teratogen might have on the developing human. First, the timing of exposure determines how the body is harmed or if, in fact, any damage occurs at all. Physical systems that are especially vulnerable early in prenatal growth, such as the heart and major limbs, may not be significantly affected later in development when they have matured more. Second, the amount of exposure determines the extent of harm that may occur. The frequency and severity of exposure to teratogens often directly predicts the extent of damage to the fetus. Moreover, hazards can interact with one another, so that limited exposures to several potential harms can have a compounding effect.

There are many kinds of potential harms. Viruses and bacteria that cause disease in the mother can cross the placental barrier to infect and damage the fetus. These include the human immunodeficiency virus (HIV) and the organisms that cause syphilis and other sexually transmitted infections. German measles (rubella) in the mother in early pregnancy can cause severe defects in the fetus, such as blindness, deafness, heart problems, and brain damage.

Certain medicinal drugs, such as aspirin and antidepressants, may harm the fetus, and maternal use of psychoactive drugs like heroin, cocaine, and marijuana can cause long-term behavioural problems or learning disabilities in the child. Moderate or heavy consumption of alcoholic beverages during pregnancy can cause serious damage to the fetus, including fetal alcohol syndrome, and use of tobacco can impair fetal growth and lead to other complications.

The mother's exposure to lead, mercury, polychlorinated biphenyls (PCBs), and other industrial chemicals—through, for example, drinking contaminated water or eating fish from polluted waters—can harm prenatal growth and cause birth defects because these substances are absorbed by the fetus. Finally, nutritional deficiencies in the mother's diet can harm the growing fetus. Folic acid deficiency, for example, can lead to neural tube defects such as spina bifida. As knowledge of potential hazards to prenatal development grows, expectant mothers and their partners can better develop healthy habits that increase their chances of having a healthy baby.

The World of the Newborn: The full-term newborn, or neonate, has remarkable competencies for surviving in the outside world. Many of these are reflexes—automatic or involuntary responses. The sucking reflex, for example, causes newborns to begin to suck on anything touching their lips, and the rooting reflex causes them to turn their heads toward anything that touches the cheek and to attempt to suck on it. A surprisingly strong grasping reflex causes newborns to clasp their hands around anything put in their palms. In addition, newborns are highly attentive to the events around them. They look toward moving objects and listen closely to the sound of voices—especially their mother's voice, which they heard inside the womb. These characteristics deepen parents' emotional attachments to their newborns.

Caring for a newborn can be challenging, however, because it takes time for the child to become physiologically organised for life outside the womb. Parents observe this in the newborn's erratic sleeping patterns, unexplained fussiness, and unpredictable behavioural states—for example, changing from focused attention to deep sleep almost unexpectedly.

Adapting to life with a newborn is especially difficult for parents if the child is premature (born too early) or of low birth weight, because such newborns can require days or weeks of hospitalisation until they are ready to go home.

Advances in medical technology have increased the survival rates of children born very early. Most hospitals now allow parents to become involved in the care of their newborn so that family relationships can begin to form.

INFANCY DAYS

Although birth is the culmination of months of prenatal development, people commonly regard infancy, from birth to age two, as a time of beginnings. Infancy is when personality, social attachments, thinking, and language first take shape. In two short years, the helpless newborn grows into a toddler with an impressive range of physical, cognitive, and social skills.

Physical Development: The child grows faster in infancy than at any later time. Physical size increases and body proportions change as the top-heavy newborn evolves into a toddler with a body more closely resembling an adult. These changes in body proportions help to account for significant improvements in motor coordination, balance, and physical dexterity during infancy.

By the age of two, children can walk, run, jump in place, pick up small objects with their fingers, and build towers with blocks. Improvements in sensory ability also contribute to these accomplishments. Changes in the eye, ear, and other sense organs, together with developments in brain organisation, enable two-year-old to see, hear, and respond with greater discrimination than ever before.

The brain grows significantly in size and complexity in infancy. Although most of the brain's neurons (nerve cells) develop prenatally, organisation and interconnection of these neurons depends significantly on experiences after birth. Normal visual stimulation, for example, organises the infant brain's visual pathways to facilitate proper sight and perception.

Hearing everyday sounds and speech organises the brain regions related to sound and language. Thus, ordinary experiences over a broad period of time naturally provoke the developing brain to organise itself. There is no evidence that special or rare experiences are required for the brain's growth, or that enhanced early stimulation will yield improvements in brain capacity. However, infants who are deprived of normal stimulation and care are at risk of impaired brain development.

Normal physical development in infancy requires a nutritionally adequate diet, immunisations to guard against infectious diseases, and protections from environmental hazards (such as lead-based paints) and from dangerous drugs. Infants also need the vigilant attention of caregivers because accidents are the leading cause of injury and death for the very young. Finally, early vision and hearing screenings are imperative to identify any deficiencies that could deprive the developing brain of essential stimulation.

Cognitive Development: The dramatic pace of brain development in infants helps to explain their hunger for stimulation. Infants crave novelty and become bored with familiarity. They integrate knowledge from different senses, such as looking toward the source of an interesting sound. They can make sophisticated inferences about an object's shape, size, and physical properties just by watching its actions. These characteristics illustrate one of the most important features of cognitive development. Young children do not passively wait to be taught about the world's mysteries. The young mind is remarkably active and self-organising.

Infants' cognitive abilities develop rapidly. After only a few months infants can mentally group similar objects into a simple category, such as round, square, soft, or flat. They also show special interest in objects that look or feel different from familiar ones. Early in the first year, infants appreciate object permanence—the concept that objects and people continue to exist even when they cannot be seen.

Infants' long-term memory for specific events is very fragile at a few months of age. However, studies have demonstrated that infants can retrieve memories when given appropriate cues, such as sounds and objects that were present at the original event. By eight or nine months of age, the memory abilities of infants have improved. For example, they can imitate behaviour they witnessed a day earlier. By the end of the first year, infants can discriminate between male and female faces (based on features like hair length) and between different categories of animals (understanding, for example, that a parakeet is more like a hawk than a horse).

Cognitive growth is also motivated by infants' fascination with "making things happen" through their own efforts, by which they learn about causes and effects. Parents observe their baby's mealtime experiments with gravity (dropping food on the floor), physical force (pushing a toy against the baby food jar), and movement (pulling on a tablecloth to reach the milk). Beneath these apparently casual activities is an active mind that is learning about the consequences of actions.

Infancy is also when the basics of language development occur. At birth, infants have a natural ability—surpassing that of adults—to hear the differences between speech sounds in any of the world's languages, even sounds they have never previously heard. They lose this capacity by the end of the first year, when their speech perception becomes specific to the language sounds they hear at home. By this time, their babbling has also started to become language-specific, as babies practice the speech sounds they hear and will use.

An infant's first recognisable word, usually spoken around the first birthday, is preceded by several months during which he or she clearly comprehends many simple sentences and expressions. For example, a ten-month-old baby who is asked "Where's Mommy?" will usually look in her direction. A baby's first words are not used very precisely. Depending on context and inflection, for example, a single word, "Daddy," may refer to a specific person, many people (all male adults), an inquiry ("Where is Daddy?"), an explanation ("Daddy's there"), or have other meaning. Vocabulary growth is slow early in the second year, but by 18 months a typical toddler's vocabulary begins to explode. New words are learned weekly, and later, daily. By the end of the second year, most toddlers combine words into simple phrases and sentences, such as "More juice."

A toddler's everyday social interaction with caregivers provides rich opportunities for language development. Adults' "baby talk"—marked by a high and varied pitch, simple words, and a slower rate of speech—is well suited to early language learning. When caregivers talk to toddlers about shared experiences, they contribute to vocabulary growth, conversational skills, and understanding and memory of events.

Social and Emotional Development: Close relationships with people are vital for the infant's personality and social growth. Even newborns seem to appreciate the importance of people. They pay special attention to faces and voices, and social stimulation provokes greater interest and emotion than does interaction with objects.

In early infancy, social relationships are important for helping to manage the baby's emotions and temperamental individuality. Young infants exhibit a variety of emotions—including joy, distress, surprise, interest, and sadness—but have difficulty managing these feelings, and rely on caregivers to soothe and regulate emotional arousal. As they later develop a broader emotional repertoire, they turn to adults for cues about situations that might be scary or dangerous, such as encountering an unfamiliar adult. In this way, emotional development is guided by parents and other care-givers.

Young children vary in their temperamental qualities. Inborn characteristics like mood, adaptability, activity level, and "soothability" affect the child's responses to situations, emotional tendencies, and tolerance of stress. Care-givers influence personality development by how they respond to a baby's temperament.

Sensitive caregivers who can adapt their childrearing practices to the child's individuality—such as providing a high-activity-level child with plenty of opportunities to expend energy—encourage more positive, constructive personality characteristics, regardless of temperament. By contrast, when caregivers cannot accommodate to a child's temperamental qualities, children may develop behavioural difficulties because their emerging personality conflicts with social expectations and demands.

As infants mature in the early months, they participate more with their parents in face-to-face play that has no other purpose than mutual delight. This coordinated interaction of gazing, smiles, vocalisations, movement, and touch is built on the baby's recognition of the parents as familiar people, and the parents' awareness that their child responds in special ways to them alone. By the end of the first year, infants have developed emotional attachments to their parents (and other regular caregivers) and rely on them for security and confidence, especially in unfamiliar settings.

Attachments can vary in their degree of security for the baby. Secure attachments arise from sensitive, responsive care and provide a foundation of trust that an infant may generalise to other relationships. Insensitive or inconsistent care may instead cause infants to develop insecure attachments that are characterised by uncertainty or distrust in the attachment figure. Secure attachments are thus an important foundation for social and personality development arising from the baby's experience of early care. Sensitive, responsive care remains a continuing need throughout childhood.

Social relationships in infancy also influence the growth of self-awareness and self-understanding. A baby's awareness of the responses of other people contributes to a dawning sense of individuality. In the second year, toddlers become capable of self-recognition in a mirror and begin to adopt others' evaluations of them when feeling proud or guilty (for example, "Me big!" after a mother has applauded her child's success at using a spoon). In these and other ways, close relationships help very young children begin to understand who they are.

EARLY CHILDHOOD

The word infancy comes from the Latin word infans, meaning "without speech." Although children are indeed speaking words by age two, early childhood (ages two to six) is when language revolutionises children's thinking, remembering, and understanding of emotions, self, and the social world. Once regarded as "egocentric," pre-schoolers are now viewed by developmental scientists as deeply interested in how others' beliefs, feelings, and desires compare with their own.

Physical Development: Between ages two and six, children with adequate nutrition and health care typically grow 8 cm. (3 in) and add nearly 2 kg. (4.4 lbs) annually, but the range of variation for normal height and weight is broad. Rapid physical development is combined with changes in body proportions, strength, and coordination that enable pre-schoolers to skip, throw a ball, ride a tricycle, draw with a crayon, and perform other feats that are beyond any toddler. Children become taller, slimmer, heavier, and less top-heavy and, by age six, their body proportions resemble those of adults. However, their high activity level and exuberance, together with limited judgement, make accident prevention a major concern of care-givers.

As the brain continues to mature throughout early childhood, there are dramatic improvements in thinking, language, memory, emotion regulation, and self-control. For example, early childhood witnesses growth in brain areas governing self-regulation, which is why six-year-olds are so much more skilled than toddlers at sitting still and playing games like "Simon Says." Advances in memory, language, and other abilities are also based on the connection and refinement of brain pathways in early childhood.

Cognitive Development: The mind's growth during early childhood is unmistakable. Pre-schoolers constantly ask "Why?" They animatedly share the day's events and proudly display their knowledge of animals and other interests. Their mushrooming language ability supports further cognitive growth, giving them access to the knowledge of others and enabling them to share their thoughts and learn more. Adults are inevitably impressed with the fantastic imaginations of Pre-schoolers and with their deep interest in understanding the world, especially people.

The intellectual achievements of early childhood are remarkable, although many abilities remain limited or only partially developed. In the area of memory, Pre-schoolers' recall of specific past experiences is notoriously unreliable and incomplete. For example, they may recall events out of sequence or fail to remember key parts. Yet a skilled questioner can often help Pre-schoolers reveal accurate memories by asking them about specific parts of an experience and helping them reconstruct the event.

One reason why Pre-schoolers sometimes seem to have poor memories is that they often remember only the features of an experience that capture their attention, rather than aspects adults consider relevant. For example, a child who attended a baseball game might remember eating peanuts, standing up, and singing, but not who won the game. Pre-schoolers are better at remembering the general sequence of familiar events. For example, four-years old understand that going to the grocery store involves getting a shopping cart, selecting food, paying the cashier, and loading the groceries in the car.

Pre-schoolers are adept at solving practical problems, like moving a step stool in front of the sink to reach the faucet. Most lack the logical reasoning skills that support formal or abstract problem solving. Simple mathematics is beyond them, for example, because of the mental flexibility and abstraction it requires. Nevertheless, they show remarkable solutions to informal challenges. For example, many five-year-olds can figure out how a bird's nest is constructed, especially with an adult's guidance, by observing its ingredients and imagining where the bird found them. Proper use of numbers comes gradually. At age three, most children have difficulty following basic number rules. They may count an object more than once and may count in the wrong order. By age five, most children have mastered these basic principles of counting.

One of the compelling interests of young children is people–especially what goes on in people's minds. As children mature, they begin to grasp how mental processes work. At age two, children have a simple awareness that intentions guide people's actions. At age three, children can appreciate how beliefs and desires are subjective, private mental experiences that differ between people. By age five, children realise that thoughts may not accurately reflect reality—people can be mistaken or fooled. As young children continue to grow and develop their "theory of mind," they can better understand others and themselves, and become more skilled social partners.

Early childhood is a time of amazing strides in language development. By age three, children are already putting words together into simple sentences, mastering grammar, and undergoing a "vocabulary explosion" that will result, by age six, in a vocabulary of more than 10,000 words. Pre-schoolers acquire new words at a staggering rate—five to six new words daily—as they employ intuitive rules for understanding the word meanings on their first exposure to them. Young children also show considerable grammatical awareness in how they put words together into sentences.

Sometimes this causes children to over-extend the meanings of words beyond their appropriate use or to over regularise grammatical rules by applying them to irregular forms. For example, a four-year-old might say "Grandpa bought a toy for me," misapplying the rule for adding ed to make a verb past tense. When adults demonstrate correct usage—for example, by responding "Really, Grandpa bought a toy for you?"—children master grammar more rapidly.

Social and Emotional Development: The cognitive accomplishments of early childhood—particularly, communication through language and a developing concept of how others think and feel—transform Pre-schoolers' social interaction and self-understanding. By age two or three, a child's emotional repertoire broadens to include self-referential emotions such as pride, guilt, shame, and embarrassment, and the evaluations of others begin to influence the preschooler's self-concept. The three-year-old's insistence on "doing it myself" also reveals developing self-awareness. Throughout early childhood, Pre-schoolers correct themselves as they are drawing, tying shoelaces, and performing other skills, demonstrating their growing capacity for self-monitoring and their motivation to be competent.

Beginning at age three, moreover, Pre-schoolers begin to remember events in terms of their personal significance. These "autobiographical memories" help to provide a continuous sense of identity throughout life. Awareness of being a boy or a girl is also an important facet of developing identity, as children begin to enact gender roles and stereotypes around age three. By the end of the preschool years, children are adept at describing themselves not only in physical terms (big, fast) but also in psychological terms (friendly, shy).

The emotional attachments of young children to their parents (and other caregivers) remain a cornerstone of psychological well-being in early childhood. But as young children develop their sense of self and learn to negotiate, compromise, resist, and assert their own preferences, they are likely to come into conflict with their care-givers. At the same time, care-givers increasingly set limits and expect compliance, based on the child's developing capacities for self-control.

The parents' approach to discipline and to conflict resolution has important effects on the quality of the parent-child relationship and the child's early personality growth. Generally, developmental scientists have found that when parents frequently exercise power and authority to overcome their children's assertiveness, the children comply but are also likely to become angry and frustrated—and to be defiant when the parent is not present. Often, children of parents who use physical punishment act aggressively toward others. Parental strategies that emphasise communicating firm and consistent expectations and their rationale, as well as listening receptively to the child's views, foster the child's cooperation and a more harmonious parent-child relationship. An affectionate parent-child relationship, in turn, enhances the child's compliance and cooperation. Young children are motivated to comply with an adult's expectations when they are emotionally committed to maintaining a strong, warm relationship with that person.

Conflicts with others can be valuable sources of social and emotional understanding for young children. Nothing focuses a child's attention on what another is thinking or feeling more than the realisation that conflict must be resolved. For example, a young boy who turns to his mother for comfort after a fight with his brother may learn from her why his brother felt as he did. With such guidance, Pre-schoolers can better comprehend and empathise with other people's feelings and perspectives. This knowledge also helps them cope with their own emotions and deal with future conflicts.

MIDDLE CHILDHOOD

During middle childhood, from about ages 6 to 12, children acquire heightened capacities for judgment, reasoning, social understanding, emotion management, and self-awareness. At the same time, the social world of middle childhood broadens beyond the family to include the school, neighbourhood, peer group, and other influences. Children begin to perceive themselves in multiple roles and relationships besides those of the family, even though family relationships remain central.

Physical Development: In contrast to the rapid physical development of the earlier years, children grow more slowly and gradually during middle childhood. Even so, children who are well nourished gain about 6 cm. (2.5 in) in height and 1.8 to 2.3 kg. (4 to 5 lb) in weight each year. Children typically become slimmer as their body proportions change. Muscular growth and better coordination enable children to ride a bicycle, run faster and for longer distances, participate in organised sports, write neatly with a pencil, learn to sew, and acquire other skills that require greater strength, endurance, or precision than younger children can manage. Brain growth contributes to these physical achievements, especially as brain pathways governing sensation, action, and thinking become speedier.

Children vary in physical size, weight, and coordination. During middle childhood, these differences can affect social and personal adjustment as children compare their characteristics and capabilities to those of their peers. Although many variations in physique are attributable to individual differences in rate of maturation and are not necessarily enduring, some can foreshadow potentially long-term difficulties for children. Childhood obesity, for example, can signal a broader problem if it arises from inactivity (such as watching too much television) or poor eating habits. Moreover, obesity in middle childhood can be damaging and self-perpetuating if it causes a child to be teased and rejected by friends and to develop a self-image as unattractive, inactive, and isolated.

Cognitive Development: It is no accident that throughout most of the world, children begin formal education at age six or seven. The intellectual skills of middle childhood are well suited for school. Children become capable of reasoning logically and systematically, whether about a lunar eclipse, chess, or the motives of story characters. Their thinking is also more fluid and flexible: A grade-schooler can follow a line of reasoning—say, solving an equation—and, realising that an error has been made, mentally reverse course and start from the beginning again. A grasp of logical principles helps older children readily understand science, math, and many other subjects. They can concentrate better, and longer, than before.

Older children also begin to master and enjoy their intellect. They become more consciously aware of their mental processes—such as what it takes to memorise a spelling list or remember a specific past event—and can deliberately enlist their cognitive powers to accomplish their goals. For example, they enlist memory strategies that strengthen their recall of experiences and information. Older children seem to think more quickly than younger children (and many adults) because they know how to do so. They spontaneously monitor and evaluate their progress and thus correct and improve their work. They are more likely to use external aids, such as writing things down, to help them think. These qualities make older children more capable and motivated learners.

Many other cognitive skills also improve. Reading and mathematical ability advances significantly, along with vocabulary and grammatical skills. Many children begin to learn a second-language in middle childhood. Children's knowledge of many specific topics that interest them expands dramatically, whether of planets, dinosaurs, or rock stars. Capacities to read music and master a musical-instrument grow significantly. Although children at this stage are still rather concrete thinkers—that is, abstractions and hypothetical issues are hard for them to understand—they have the intellectual skills to function competently in the adult world.

The cognitive achievements of middle childhood both contribute to school success and are, in part, a result of schooling. Effective classroom instruction strengthens children's capacity for logical, objective reasoning through well-designed activities that promote active learning. Children also benefit from group projects as peers sharpen each other's intellectual skills. However, intellectual growth in middle childhood is not just a result of the growth of the mind in combination with classroom practices; parental support is another crucial ingredient. Parents who value learning, have high expectations for their children's academic success, and supervise homework and other school-related activities contribute significantly to their children's cognitive growth and school success.

Because learning is more formalised in middle childhood, achievement is evaluated more objectively and publicly. School-children receive formal and informal evaluations of their work in the classroom and in school-wide achievement testing. Consequently, children quickly learn how their abilities measure up with their peers and with teacher expectations. In comparing themselves to their peers, older children develop a more balanced view of their intellectual strengths and weaknesses. In contrast to optimistic Pre-schoolers, who tend to believe they can improve their intellectual skills through effort and practice, older children begin to view their intellectual abilities as relatively permanent traits. They may conclude that they are "good at" some subjects but that they "can't do" others. These self-evaluations tend to make older children less confident and more self-critical, causing some of them to give up too early when faced with intellectual tasks that are challenging but within their reach.

BEYOND CHILDHOOD

The onset of puberty marks the beginning of adolescence. Physical growth and development, including sexual maturation, is an important part of adolescence. But this period of life is also shaped by other changes: entry into middle schools that are larger and more impersonal than elementary schools, peer groups that include older children, and greater independence in extracurricular activities. Adolescents achieve new cognitive skills permitting highly abstract thinking, engage in new kinds of social intimacy with peers, and embark on a search for identity that results in greater awareness of the self. Adolescence includes risks for psychological turmoil, but most children make their way through this period without undue stress.

People continue to develop through adolescence and, indeed, throughout adulthood. As people age, they may continue to be influenced by childhood experiences, positively or negatively. The lasting influence of childhood on a person's relationships, self-esteem, and well-being is one reason why efforts to improve the lives of children are so important. Few developmental scientists believe, however, that one's behaviour and personality as an adult are inevitably determined by earlier influences. Childhood sets the stage, but a person's traits may be changed by subsequent events and experiences.

❑

3
TEENAGERS' PROBLEMS

He's become so secretive and moody and just wants to be with his friends all the time.

She's become so argumentative and abusive. Any time we ask her to do anything she starts World War Three in the house.

Sound familiar? Becoming a parent of a teenager can be a troubled and stormy time. The young open child who chatted happily to you can suddenly become this argumentative and resentful teenager who challenges everything you say. Teenagers can become secretive and suspicious and you can feel redundant and locked out of their lives.

In addition, you can be full of fears for your teenager. There are so many pressures on teenagers to be involved in drugs and alcohol or to become sexually active at too young an age.

With their increasing independence, you can also fear for their safety, worrying that they might be attacked or placed in very unsafe situations. You struggle with setting boundaries and limits with a teenager who can resent your authority as a parent.

Parents are usually in their forties or fifties at the time and may be going through their own midlife crisis. At this stage of life parents are often wondering about the direction of their own lives and careers, sometimes feeling that life has passed them by. Having teenagers who seem to have endless opportunities and who appear ungrateful can stir up a lot of emotion in parents, even causing them to feel envious.

Alternatively, parents may be looking forward to a quieter period in their life, only for this to be rudely disturbed by the arrival of a noisy and demanding teenager. In this context it is understandable for parents to react negatively to this stormy period, to lose sight of the bigger picture and miss out on the enjoyable aspects of parenting a teenager.

It's Difficult for Teenagers Too: The transition from child to adult is difficult for teenagers also. So many changes occur in these short years that it is not surprising that they feel at times confused, frightened and lacking in confidence. Physically, their bodies grow and change in ways that might make them feel awkward and self-conscious. Emotionally, they can be subject to great mood swings as they discover the range of human emotions. From intense feelings of love and infatuation to anger and hatred, teenage emotional life can be like a roller coaster.

Physically, teenagers become fully developed and can experience intense sexual feelings that can be alarming to them, especially if they have no one to talk to about what is going on. Intellectually, teenagers also make great gains, being able to analyse things and to develop their own opinions and views. They can begin to see the inadequacies in the parental world (and often are very eloquent in pointing this out) and wonder about their role and meaning in life. Teenagers are under pressures, some of which are greater than in previous years, and need the support of their parents more than ever.

When facing the crisis of the teenage years, many parents react by trying to take control. They may become authoritarian and strict, battling with their teenagers to ensure they toe the line. Alternatively, other parents avoid their teenagers' problems and back down from every conflict, effectively giving up at trying to influence their teenagers or to be involved in their lives.

Both these approaches are problematic: the young person with authoritarian parents may rebel even more strongly, escalating the conflict, or they may go 'underground' with their problems, hiding more things from their parents. The teenager with permissive parents may feel uncared for and neglected and, without parental supervision, get involved in out-of-control and unsafe behaviours. Both approaches rob teenagers of having involved parents who can support them through the difficulties they face.

A Time of Opportunity: Rather than seeing the teenage years as solely problem years, try to see them as full of opportunity. During these years parents have the opportunity to form a different relationship with their child, one that is more adult and equal. Teenage rebellion is not a personal attack on your authority but a necessary stage for teenagers to go through as they forge their separate identity. If you remain curious and interested in this process, you can help them think through their values and ideas.

By staying involved in your teenagers' lives you can get to know them in a different light—as young adults rather than children. Many parents report how satisfying it can be to begin to have adult conversations with their teenagers. In addition by staying involved you can share in their achievements and discoveries as they mature and grow up. You can appreciate and enjoy their excitement as they face a world full of opportunity and you can have the pleasure of being one of their closest supports as they take on the world.

In the difficult times, try to remember that parenting is a long-term task. By staying involved and being firm when needed, you can chart a course through the difficult times so that you can be there as your teenagers grow into young adults of whom you can be proud.

Teenagers are at a time of life when they are separating from their parents. They are becoming their own people, with different ideas and values. Though this is healthy, it can bring them into conflict with their parents and lead to a stormy time for all this period can be difficult for parents. Teenagers can become challenging and demanding. At times they can become disrespectful and even abusive to their parents.

It is not surprising that parents, hurt and bewildered by these exchanges, can react negatively by criticising, lecturing, rowing and even lashing out at their teenagers. This can lead to unpleasant scenes, like that described above, leaving both teenager and parent upset and hurt. So how can a parent handle this conflict? How can you stop things from escalating to a full-blown row? The first thing you can do is press the pause button. Rather than reacting to a situation or 'flying off the handle', pause and ask yourself the following questions:

What is the best way to manage this situation?

What way do I want to respond?

What result do I want?

In conflictual situations, pressing the pause button may mean taking a deep breath and calming down when you feel yourself getting angry or about to react to a situation. It can be best not to continue the argument, which may lead to hurtful things being said, and to set a time later to talk things through when everyone is calmer.

Connecting with Your Teenager: *When my children got older, I felt redundant. They had their own friends and lives. It became harder to understand them.*

Parents Matter: Often parents have the sense of being out of touch with their teenager. Teenagers get caught up with their own friends and interests, and it is easy to feel distant from them and that you don't matter to them any more. Yet teenagers still really need their parents. Though they are growing up and separating from the family, they still need support, guidance and encouragement.

They need parents who remain involved and interested in their lives. Young people need adults who can be there to coach them and act as their 'co-pilot' as they negotiate the problems they face in their lives. If you are unsure about the importance of your role in your teenager's life, you only have to consider the extensive research showing that teenagers whose parents stay connected and supportively involved in their lives are much more likely to grow into healthy, successful adults with fewer problems.

Researchers have also found that children whose parents discuss issues such as drugs with them are 36 per cent less likely to experiment with drugs than children whose parents do not have these discussions. Staying involved in your teenagers' lives or having a connection with them does not mean knowing everything about them or learning things so you can control them. Teenagers need their privacy and distance and it would be inappropriate for them to reveal all their innermost secrets to their parents.

Rather, having a connection with teenagers is about knowing the ordinary details in their lives that are important to them, such as the names of their friends, their routine at school, the position of their team in the league, what their favourite dinner is, etc. When you know these mundane and ordinary details about your teenagers lives, not only does it mean that you are sharing in their lives, but it gives you an opportunity to influence them positively about other important matters such as drug-taking and safety.

Building a connection with a child or teenager is not something that can be rushed or fitted into a busy schedule. The most important decision you can make is to set time aside when you can talk and be with your teenager in a relaxed way. This does not have to be a special activity or trip (though these can help). Mundane, ordinary activities, such as watching TV together, driving to school, mealtimes, washing up together, all can become activities where parent and child are happily chatting to one another.

Some parents find routine events of the day particularly helpful times to talk and listen to their children, such as when they come in from school, at mealtimes, or late at night just before they go to bed. Many families agree to make some of these times special, such as Sunday dinner, when everyone makes an effort to be there.

Be Encouraging: Teenagers are often insecure and struggling with many pressures at school and from friends. The argumentative or sulky moods are only a front and they need more than ever the support and encouragement of their parents. It is important that this encouragement be given in a genuine way, as teenagers will be the first to shrug off any attention they consider to be 'phoney' or manipulative. Generally, encouragement works best with teenagers if it is matter of fact rather than 'over the top', and if it is specific and clear (whereby you clearly name what you are pleased about and how you feel about it).

Remember, each teenager is different; what gets through with one teenager will not work for another. What is important is that you find a way of providing encouragement to your teenager about routine, everyday activities. Giving compliments to teenagers in a genuine way that gets through to them can make a difference:

Noticing if your teenager tries harder at school work.

Casually thanking your teenager when he does a chore, rather than taking it for granted.

Complimenting teenagers on their appearance or what they're wearing.

Going out of your way to look for positive things does not come easily to most of us. We are not used to it, and praise can be hard to give, particularly when there has been conflict or things have not been going well with a child for some time.

But that is probably the most important time to be positive and to notice even small signs of improvement. For example, if your teenager is normally grumpy with visitors, but on one occasion, behaves more positively, you could say, 'I appreciate it when you talk with my friends, it means a lot to me when you take an interest'. Or if a teenager normally gets into a row with his sister, but on one occasion walks away, you could say, 'I was impressed with how you handled things with your sister earlier. You didn't get wound up and avoided a row.

Responding to Your Teenager's Initiative: One of the greatest opportunities to connect with teenagers is to respond to any initiatives they make to talk with or connect with you. Often they choose inopportune times, when you're busy or when you're tired or just about to go out and do something yourself. However, it's worth weighing up in these situations what is really important the tasks you're busy with or your relationship with your teenager. While you can sometimes postpone responding to your teenager, it can be really helpful to respond there and then, especially if your teenager does not usually open up or try to make a connection with you. It can be a case of making sure to 'seize the opportunity'. Consider the following examples:

If your son asks for help with homework and you're busy, try to give a little bit of time and then set aside another time to help.

If your daughter suddenly opens up one night because her boyfriend split up with her, this might be a time to postpone going to bed and to stay up and listen.

If your son wants to watch a favourite TV programme and you're reading, it might be a good idea to postpone your reading and to watch the programme with him.

If your daughter asks you a personal question when you're reading the newspaper, you can put down the newspaper for a few minutes and try to listen and answer the question.

If your son asks you for a lift, rather than lecturing him about' not being his chauffeur', use the journey as an opportunity to listen and talk to him.

What Teenagers Think About?: So what do teenagers think about? Below are the sorts of worries that teenagers have reported as most concerning them.

Will I make friends or will anyone like me?

Will anyone fancy me or ask me out?

How come I don't fit in with others?

What should I do about drugs and alcohol?

Will I do okay in the class exams?

Will I ever get a decent job?

What should I do with my life?

How can I please my parents/get them off my back?

Teenagers also Tend to have Strong Views about How they should be Parented and about, What they Want from their Parents? They want their parents to trust them and have faith in them.

They want Privacy: They want to talk to their parents about some things but they don't want to tell them everything.

Below are three styles of disempowering parenting that you can easily fall into, despite the best of intentions. Each of these styles cultivates irresponsibility in teenagers and does not prepare them for the task of being an adult.

Over-protective Parent: Doing everything for your teenagers, for example, waking them up in the morning, making their breakfast and lunch, tidying up for them, washing their clothes, covering for them when they miss homework etc.

Critical Parent: Nagging, correcting, instructing teenagers over every task without giving them space and responsibility—for example nagging them to do the learn and then standing over them while they do it, even criticising their attempts.

Permissive Parent: Giving your teenagers excessive 'space' so that you are uninvolved and have little influence in their lives (meaning they learn little from you).

Parents Caring for Themselves: There was a man working furiously in the woods trying to saw down a tree. He was making very little progress, as his saw was blunt and becoming blunter with each stroke. The man was hot and frustrated and continued to work harder and harder. A friend of his noticed what was going on and he asked him, 'Why don't you stop for a few minutes so you can sharpen your saw?'. 'Don't you see.' replied the man, 'I'm too busy sawing to take any time off.'

So many parents become martyrs to their children, devoting all their time and energy to the task of parenting, without thinking of their needs and wishes. Other parents become excessively focused on the problems and conflicts they have with their children and all their energy is spent disagreeing with their children or correcting and rowing with them.

In both these positions, not only is the parent liable to burn out from stress and exhaustion, but their parenting becomes increasingly counter-productive and negative. In the first example, the parents can become resentful and/or can become rundown, with little energy to relate to their children in a consistent, loving way. In the second, example, the correcting approach is liable to increase the power struggle between parent and teenager, and may lead to more rebellion, until either parent gives up or the teenager walks out. As the story above suggests, it is crucial to take time out to 'sharpen the saw'.

Parents should 'press the pause button' and take time to look after their won needs as well as attending to the needs of their children, When parents' own needs for care, comfort and fulfilment are met, they are freed up to attend fully to their parenting role. Children need cared-for parents as much as their parents to care for them. The best way to help your child grow upto be confident people with high self-esteem is for you as their parent to model this—that is, to take steps to value, love and priorities yourself.

You may protest that in your busy life you simply can't afford to take time out for yourself. The reality is that you can't afford not to. Think about the times you have been run down or exhausted or feeling low and how it was impossible then to do any of the 'more important' tasks. Remember the times you felt energetic and good about yourself and how easy it was too achieve things and to be kind and loving to others. A little bit of self-care goes a long way.

The Parent-Teen Relationship: How Parents can make the Most of It?

"Enjoy them now, they'll soon be teenagers!" Warnings like this from friends and relatives, together with media images of adolescents as irresponsible, rebellious troublemakers, can lead parents to expect trouble as their children enter puberty. It is a rare parent who does not approach a child's adolescence without some misgivings.

But family life does not have to be a battleground during the teenage years. Parents and teens can live together, more or less harmoniously, if parents know what to expect and are willing to make some adjustments in the way they think and act.

The purpose of these fact sheets is to help parents cope more effectively during their children's adolescence. Although this information is intended mainly for parents of teenagers, it is general enough to be useful to parents of younger children as well. The first fact sheet discussed the way teenagers develop and what parents can do to help them through this time in their life. This second fact sheet focuses on strategies parents can use to deal with typical teenage behaviour.

The Cultural Context: Teens get bad press. All too often publicity about teenagers highlights the ones in trouble: the runaways and the lawbreakers. You rarely hear about the hospital volunteers and the camp counsellors.

Teens have no status, no recognised place in our society. We no longer need them to do essential chores like milking cows or chopping wood jobs that gave them a sense of usefulness and worth. (Even when teens work part-time, their earnings are not usually necessary for their family's survival). Young people used to grow up quickly. Now we require them to be dependent and regimented until they acquire the education they need to find jobs in a technology-oriented society.

Social isolation is another problem. The trend toward smaller families, increased mobility and the high divorce rate often mean there are no relatives close by to help teens and their parents get over the rough spots. When friction develops between parent and teenager, there may be no one to turn to for help and advice, no one who can step in and defuse the situation.

Not surprisingly, parents sometimes feel overwhelmed by the stress of bringing up teenagers. But there are steps we can take to make things better. We can begin by remembering our own adolescence. Asking ourselves questions like "How much did I share with my parents?" "How critical and argumentative was I at that stage?" and "What were my worries and dreams?" can help us accept our teens' behaviour better.

Some things are true in every age and in every culture. Adolescence is always a struggle for independence it is common for teenagers to challenge their parents. Teens still cope, as we did, with major physical changes, emotional ups and downs, unfamiliar sexual stages, peer pressure, a changing identity, important life decisions and the resulting loneliness and anxiety.

The world is changing rapidly and differs in many ways from the one we grew up in. Teens today face a more complex and impersonal society. Alcohol and drugs are more easily available. Today's teens also have to worry about AIDS, violence and uncertain job prospects. The pressures on today's teens are intense. Young people have become a major target group for advertisers and media hucksters, who constantly urge them to grow up quickly and have it all now!

Family Relationships: Teens are out of balance at the same time as their parents are struggling with their own mid-life pressures. While teens are dismayed by each new pimple, parents may be agonising over each new wrinkle. While teens are thinking in terms of the time ahead and the opportunities it will bring, parents are beginning to think in terms of time remaining and the opportunities that are diminishing. While teens are gradually acquiring more personal power, parents are often beginning to confront their own limitations. Giving up power over their children may be difficult. Good parents aim at working themselves out of their job, but the difficult part is knowing how and when to let go.

Parents are not the only ones struggling with mixed feelings. As teenagers try to establish their identity, they have to adjust to the loss of childhood security and accept increasing responsibility. As our children work toward independence and self-control, our attitude to their struggle is crucial to their success. Parents and teenagers will both do much better if parents can keep a sense of perspective. When parents and teens are getting along, family life can be wonderful. Teens really are enjoyable and energising. Their wit and high spirits make them fun to be around. But when parents and teens are at odds, the teenage propensity for sullen silence and rejection can confuse and frustrate their parents. Life with teenagers is an emotional roller-coaster; certainly an adult marriage with so many ups and downs would be considered unstable. Luckily, for parents and adolescents this "on-again, off-again" relationship is normal and nothing to worry about in the long run.

Make the most of the good times with your teens. Think about your children's likeable qualities even when they're temporarily exhibiting their unlikeable ones. It is important for parents to see the instability in the relationship for what it is a necessary part of the teen's development in separating from his or her parents.

Handling Anger: Growing up is difficult sometimes and anger plays a key part in the process of separating from parents. Teens resent being dependent, but they're afraid of having to take care of themselves. They are annoyed at being treated like an adult one minute and a child the next, but they often behave inconsistently themselves. And then they bristle when you point this out to them. Understanding your teenager's anger will help you respond to it more constructively.

In a society that often appears to condone violence as a way of solving problems, we need to help our teens control their anger and express it safely especially their anger at parents. Remember that anger is a normal emotion and that other feelings like helplessness, hurt, frustration, confusion and guilt are often expressed as anger. Ask yourself: "How can a teenager in our home express anger in acceptable ways? Do we provide our teenager with any safety valve to blow off steam?" We must make it clear to our teens that yelling, cursing, hitting and other forms of aggression are unacceptable.

There are non-violent ways to work off anger: stomping off to one's room, pounding a pillow, twisting a towel, crying, talking it out, writing in a diary or doing some form of physical exercise. In helping teens to deal with their anger, the example we set is crucial.

Like younger children, teens take their cues from us. It is therefore important that we be aware of our own behaviour, so that we don't become part of the problem. Teens often like to bait their parents, and mothers and fathers who overreact can be drawn into a destructive pattern of pointless arguments. The last thing an out-of-control teen needs is an out-of-control parent. Mothers and fathers need to ask themselves "How do I behave when I'm angry at my teen? Would I want my teen to imitate me?"

Parents can work off anger using the techniques suggested above too. When you feel your temperature rising over something your child has said or done, consciously force yourself to back off. Take time out. Give yourself a chance to cool off and relax a little before confronting the issue. It will help you keep things in perspective.

The way you talk is important. In the heat of argument, if you can't help "sounding off" about your teen's behaviour, do it without attacking his or her personality. A practical approach is to start your sentences with the word 'I' followed by a statement of your feelings. "I don't like it when you use that kind of language" or "I'm really upset when you take your anger out on me." This way you will avoid laying blame. In other words, speak as you would be spoken to.

The way you listen is important too in draining off your teen's anger. It can be passive listening silence is sometimes golden. A more useful way to listen is by trying to understand what feelings lie behind your teen's actions or words. Your response should start with the word you, as in "You sound like you're pretty frustrated," or "You look like you're really fed up." We all know how important it is to feel heard and understood, especially when we are upset. Remember that you should listen twice as much as you talk.

The 'Dos' and 'Don't's of Parent-Teen Communication:

- Don't argue with the way your teen sees things. Instead, state your own case and speak from that. "I have a different opinion," "This is what I believe," and "This is the way I see it."

- Don't talk down to your teenager. There's nothing more irritating than a condescending tone.
- Don't lecture or preach. Again, this only provokes hostility. Besides, the average teenager goes "deaf" after hearing about five sentences.
- Don't set limits you can't enforce.
- Do focus on the behaviour, not the person.
- Do think ahead to what you will say and how you will say it.
- Do keep your messages clear and concise.
- Do stick to one issue at a time.

Rules and Discipline: It's normal for adolescents to try to test the rules. Because adolescents are dependent on their parents for a long time, they can build up a great deal of resentment. This resentment can be expressed by defying parental restrictions.

Some rules are non-negotiable like "Don't drink and drive" but keep these to a minimum. Parents who make a major confrontation out of every minor issue risk losing all their influence with their teenagers. In demanding quiet submission, they may unwittingly create a simmering foe. Whenever possible, state rules as guidelines rather than ultimatums. Otherwise, family life will become a series of power struggles.

Parents need to help their children make the transition from parental discipline to self-discipline. For this to happen, teens need to learn how to negotiate and how to cooperate in setting rules and solving problems. Today, as their horizons expand, teens are more often out of our sight; they need to learn how to think for themselves so they can make the right choices when parents are not around.

You can help your teen practise negotiating, and redirect energy that might be wasted in power struggles.

Successful teen-parent negotiation depends on three things:

1. Involving your teen in the process when you make rules, set limits or reach decisions.
2. Keeping as calm and rational as possible even when emotions run high. It is especially important to control your anger.
3. Using the following specific problem-solving method, which helps keep negotiations focused on the issue.

Problem solving has several steps: identifying the issue for negotiation, brainstorming solutions, evaluating and narrowing down the alternatives until you get a solution that you both can live with, making an agreement and evaluating the outcome. In matters of discipline, it is helpful to see inappropriate or unacceptable behaviour as a mistake in judgment or choice that carries consequences for your teen. If your teen behaves badly, make your feelings known immediately. Expressing sadness or disappointment about your teen's unacceptable behaviour is more constructive than expressing anger. The former leaves the problem where it belongs with your teen while the latter shifts the focus to you.

The next step would be to negotiate with the teen the appropriate consequences for the misbehaviour so that the teen can make amends and be motivated to do better in the future. By asserting themselves, parents project by word and action the message "I love you too much to stand by and see you do something hurtful. When you show me by your behaviour that you can handle things better, I'll back off." While resolving the immediate issue at hand is important, it's even more crucial for parents to take a long-range view. Their job is to help teens develop the ability to make good decisions for themselves.

Young people not only lack experience, but also often have little foresight. Parents should teach their teens to think like chess players: before they make a move, they should try to anticipate the consequences. "What will happen to me if I make this next decision or choice?" At the same time, parents should be asking themselves "What can I do in this situation to help my teen be more responsible?"

Positive Parenting: Growing up is often discouraging. Telling your teenagers "I love you" is less important than showing in tangible ways that you care. One of the best ways is by helping your teenagers believe in themselves. And teens will only believe in themselves if they know we have confidence in them. Try to recognise their efforts and the good things they do, and reassure them, at every possible opportunity, that they have the qualities we want for them. Give them the message "I don't always understand what is going on with you but I'm on your side and I have faith that you will sort things out and land on your feet."

Caring for the Care-giver: Our culture is often as unhelpful to parents as it is to teens. Parents are expected to know how to rear their children, and to do a perfect job with very little support. When our children reach adolescence, we are caught in a classic double bind. We have to give up control, but society does not allow us to relinquish responsibility. Parents are still held accountable for the behaviour of their offspring sometimes even after they've left home.

With the loss of power also comes the bittersweet experience of giving up being needed. After years of doing for our children, the fact that they can now do for themselves can bring on a sense of loss. This is especially true for parents who have put their whole heart and soul into childrearing. You have to take care of yourself through the teen years as your children begin to need you less and challenge you more. This means setting aside time, each day if possible, to fulfil your physical and emotional needs. This will restore your energy and sense of perspective.

Relationships with other adults are important. If you are a single parent, friends and other parents of teens can be valuable confidants. If you are married or involved with someone, take time out to nurture and enjoy the relationship with your partner. Marriages can often come under stress during this stage. We need to take care of ourselves and sustain our relationships if we want to provide stability to our teens during this turbulent time in their lives.

Where to Turn for Help? Every parent feels overwhelmed from time to time. If you feel your family life is continually in turmoil or if you are always worried about your teens, you can reach out to other parents, as parents have always done, for ideas and support. You can look for family life education groups or groups for parents with special needs. There is also a great deal of family life education material available in audio, video and printed form. Similar material for people of different cultural backgrounds is beginning to become available. You can also ask your school, doctor or clergy for names of agencies where you can get professional counselling and parenting advice.

COORDINATING CHILDCARE, EDUCATION AND WORK

This research explores how coordinating childcare and education services for all the children in a family is central to reconciling work and family life. Christine Skinner, of the University of York, interviewed 40 mothers living within two separate areas in a middle-sized English city. She examined how parents coordinated getting one or more children between home, school, pre-school education, and childcare in a way that fitted with work commitments and she shows how co-ordination affected mothers' ability and willingness to work. The study found that:

- Children had to be picked up and dropped off safely and efficiently from home, childcare or education at fixed times of the day in order for parents to ensure a seamless package of care that dovetailed with their working hours.

- The number and timing of these fixed times varied depending upon the parents' (mainly mothers') working hours and the number and types of educational/childcare services used.
- Parents' own preferences for particular childcare services could make co-ordinating arrangements more complex. But complexity also increased where there was more than one child in the family and particularly children of different ages, as they used different services, often with different opening times.
- Working mothers relied on a mixture of formal, informal and back-up support to manage these arrangements. Non-working mothers managed picking up and dropping off themselves.
- Contrary to expectations, full-time working mothers had the least complex arrangements and part-time working mothers the most complex.
- Many non-working mothers believed coordination was too difficult to manage with work commitments and this deterred them from taking paid work. However, some mothers did prefer to 'be there' to pick up children from school themselves.
- One of the most difficult times to manage was moving between statutory part-time pre-school education and formal childcare in private nurseries. These services were institutionally separate, operated different opening times, were some distance apart and offered no support in transporting children between the two services.
- Fathers played an important role in transporting children, particularly where mothers worked full-time. This support was additional to, or separate from the care provided by fathers at atypical times (early morning/evenings/weekends).

Background: We know a great deal about the use of formal and informal childcare and the shortfalls in provision facing mothers who want to return to paid work. But much less is known about how childcare and educational services for all the children in the family need to be coordinated to enable parents, and especially mothers, to do paid work, or how these arrangements may deter mothers from working. This tends to be a hidden activity, wrapped up in the daily routine of family life. This research interviewed 40 mothers - seven working full-time, 21 working part-time and 12 not working—about how they managed these arrangements during term-time.

Coordinating Arrangements: The study identified critical times in the day when parents had to get themselves to and from work and their children to and from childcare and education. These affected not just the daily journeys made by individual family members, but also how these journeys had to be synchronised effectively to ensure there were no delays. For example, any delay in the journey from home to school would create a delay in the subsequent journey from school to work. Synchronising such journeys was crucial, both for the parents to maintain a good work record and to ensure the continuity of children's care.

The mother took the major responsibility. In the mornings and evenings she travelled with the children to and from the home, school, nursery, the childminder's house and her workplace. The childminder also picked up the older child from school in the afternoon and then looked after him until the evening. Thus, this family had three 'coordination points' to manage: morning, post-school and evening. The parents could not manage all three by themselves and had to rely on the childminder to pick their older child up from school, but still had to plan and organise this.

How did Parents Manage? The working mothers in the study relied on a network of individuals offering informal, formal and backup support with transporting children that was often *additional* to formal childcare.

For example, six of the seven full-time working mothers used full-time formal childcare, yet they also had to rely on informal or formal support in transporting children at least once a day. All 21 of the part-time working mothers used either formal or informal childcare, but 13 also relied on support from others with transporting children. Informal and backup support was provided by family (including fathers), friends and neighbours.

Nannies, childminders, childminders' husbands and out-of-school-clubs provided formal support with transporting children whereas no support was given by private nurseries or school nurseries. Backup support was arranged to cover exceptional events and to 'step in' when other regular support with transporting children failed. Non-working mothers managed without other support.

At its simplest, support involved fathers or others taking children to and from care/education, but within this, more elaborate coordination strategies could be involved, including:

- Parents working different hours to one another so one was always available.
- Fathers adjusting working hours to help with transporting children (leaving work early or taking shorter lunch breaks).
- Mothers restricting their hours of work to atypical evening/weekend hours.
- Parents relying on flexi-time or flexible work arrangements.
- Parents relying on the goodwill of employers and work colleagues to release them from work so they could take children to and from care.
- Booking and paying for additional formal childcare as a backup that may never be used.
- Splitting the weekly childcare for a single child across similar providers (using two instead of one private nursery for example) because one offered more extended opening hours.

Many of these strategies were used in combination and altered over time in response to children's changing educational and childcare needs. The families living in the more affluent Area A used more support than those living in the less affluent Area B. But this was closely related to more mothers in Area A working daytime hours (between 8am-6pm) and thus being less available to pick up children. Mothers in Area B were more likely to work atypical hours.

The Impact on Mothers' Working: Twelve mothers in the study were not working. Five specifically identified the following as deterring them from working:

- the inflexible nature of pre-school education;
- the inflexibility of employment to fit around pre-school and primary school education; and
- transportation problems: either a lack of access to efficient public or private transport when mothers needed it, or lack of support from others to take children to and from education or childcare. Some mothers, however, also stated a preference to 'be there' to pick up children from school themselves.

It is hard to be sure which of these factors, if any, carried the most weight as a barrier to employment. Children's age (rather than simply the numbers of children in the family) were important as different forms of education and childcare were needed, often in combination. This made arrangements both more complex and time-consuming as children needed to be taken to and from different care settings. Lack of support from others or lack of access to efficient transport also increased the 'time costs'.

Mothers also identified childcare costs as a barrier to employment; these increased in direct relationship to the numbers and ages of children in the family. Even so, it seemed that time costs were equally if not more important than childcare costs. For example, as one mother who was actively seeking a job explained:

> *"Cost definitely, but also as I say, it has been up to the dropping off factor because I don't drive, I'm being practical, I probably won't be able to run around all over the place, take one child to nursery and then the other to school, and get on to work."*

Six mothers said they were postponing returning to work until all their children were in school full-time. When all the children were old enough to go to the same school coordinating arrangements would be simpler and the journey times would reduce, potentially making it easier to return to work. However, these non-working mothers appeared to have limited choices for working in the future; first, because they wanted to dovetail their working hours around the school day so they could still 'be there' to pick up children from school themselves and, second, because they could not rely on fathers to provide support with transport or care in the evenings/weekends. Four of these non-working mothers were lone parents; in the other eight cases the fathers worked long hours into the evenings/ weekends or away from home.

Conclusion: This small-scale study found that parents, particularly mothers, were 'running around in circles'; not only were they doing the 'school run', but the 'pre-school nursery run', the 'childcare run' and the 'work run'. The main points that emerge from these interviews were:

- Coordinating arrangements is a skilled activity. It involves synchronising childcare, pre-school and primary school education with both parents' work commitments, their conditions of employment and the availability of formal and informal support with transporting children at critical times.
- Coordinating arrangements is as important as service provision. The experiences of these 40 mothers with access to the same formal childcare services shows that it was not necessarily lack of childcare that

deterred mothers from working, but the complexity of the arrangements needed in families with at least one child under five years of age.

- Coordinating arrangements is about reducing time costs. Parents, particularly mothers, were always trying to reduce the time costs associated with coordinating paid work, childcare and education.
- Fathers played an important role in enabling mothers to work, either by looking after children themselves to help reduce childcare costs or by providing informal support with transporting children to help reduce time costs.

The researcher suggests that thinking about childcare, work and education has become compartmentalised and split. More radical ways of thinking about parents' and children's needs could include:

- Tackling the lack of coordination between pre-school education and childcare, perhaps by providing integrated childcare provision within locally based schools.
- Dealing with the culture of working long hours, particularly for men.
- Recognising the needs of children and parents for efficient transport services.

CAREER IN ARMED FORCES

The most difficult stage in a teenager's life comes when it is time to contemplate professional goals or chalk out a career path. Many teenagers, out of high school and college, are confused and aimless about what they want to do in life. Children come in social contact with doctors or teachers often, so that they may subconsciously think of these professions as obvious career options. But, away from such mainstream professions, there are as many off-beat professions today as there are ideas floating around. At such times, as parents of a teenager, you have to be aware of the various career options yourselves so that you can guide your son or daughter well.

Here, we will dwell over one such career option – the Armed Forces. It is a matter of honour and pride to join the Armed Forces as these personnel are looked upon as saviours or defenders of nations and its people. It is one of the few noble professions left today.

The Armed Forces comprise three arms or services, that of the Army, Navy and Air Force. Apart from defending the borders from external threats, the Armed Forces are often involved in humanitarian missions like the UN Peacekeeping forces and in disaster management. In the event of earthquakes, floods or avalanches, the Army, Navy and Air Force are the first to reach the disaster-prone areas for search and rescue missions. In the recent tsunami disaster, the Indian Navy did women service in sending its ships and its men with food and medicines to Sri Lanka for relief operations.

The Indian Military Academy's Chetwood Hall bears an inscription, which reads: "The safety, honour and welfare of your country comes first, always and every time. The honour, welfare and comfort of the men you command, come next. Your own ease, comfort and safety comes last, always and every time." That truly epitomises what a solider stands for and what he should be. Selfless service for the nation and its people is a soldier's brief, which he is trained to follow unfailingly.

But, apart from that, the military also offers a great opportunity for growth and a good life. Today, even women are welcome in the Armed Forces in education, logistics, air traffic control and legal branches. Let us see what you stand to gain by joining the Armed Forces.

1. *Head start:* In the Armed Forces, you get to begin your career early in life. Candidates begin their career and training when they are anywhere between 15– 20 years of age, of course, eligibility varies from country

to country. Some countries have conscription or compulsory enrolment, but most modern democracies do not have such a provision.

The training period can be anywhere from one to three years, again depending on your nationality. Aspirants can join as officers or in non-officer cadres as ratings, but both follow different career patterns. The officers, of course, are entitled to greater privileges and perks. An advantage of this early head start in career is that after 10-15 years of service, you are still young enough to choose a career outside the Armed Forces, if you so desire. Moreover, the military training and service, by its very nature highly equips you for other jobs, say in managerial positions. Naval personnel can make a smooth transition to Merchant Navy and Air Force pilots can shift to commercial airlines without much ado.

2. ***Training:*** Training and education in most defence academies is free or, at least, highly subsidised. Considering the prohibitive costs of education in other streams, this is quite a scream. Academies around the world have tie-ups with university programmes and along with military training you stand to get a graduate degree or a diploma.

   Military training lays great emphasis on physical fitness and discipline. In India's National Defence Academy, every cadet's study table has Rudyard Kipling's inspirational poem, 'If' framed. That singularly epitomises what the academy training seeks to achieve.

   As part of the training, you will get to indulge in a wide variety of sports–from sailing and mountaineering to horse-riding and rifle shooting. Later, into the service you can continue with the adventure sports either as a hobby or take it up seriously as a profession. The silver medalist in shooting in Olympics 2003, Major Raghvendra Singh Rathore is a professional archer apart from being an Army officer. Indeed, it was his Army training and coaching which has been instrumental in his success.

3. *Leadership Skills:* Soldiering is all about facing situations whether it is waging wars, encountering militants or going on humanitarian missions. Soldiers have to rise up to difficult challenges, offer succour and battle with life and death—all this amidst great expectations from people. If you relish challenges and like to live on the edge of life, then this is the job for you.

   Life in the Armed Forces also gears you to rise above individual aspirations, forget differences and work as a team towards a common aim. It calls for great leadership skills and fosters the spirit of camaraderie which shall stand in good stead in any walk of life.

4. *Broadening of Horizons (Lateral education):* Armed Force personnel get posted in a variety of places – islands, forests, mountains and even deserts. They come in contact with varied flora and fauna, heritage, cuisines, people and culture—which is like lateral education for their children and families. They get to dine with the kings and sup with the commoners, so to say. Such kind of living makes them truly cosmopolitan. After a while, the distinction of race, caste and creed disappears and they assume truly homogenous identities.

   In a country like India, with its diversities, inter-caste marriages in the Armed Forces are rampant and you get to see national integration at its best, here.

5. *Travel:* While they get posted in interesting and remote places, the personnel also get great opportunities to travel. The Indian Navy's motto has been: "Join the navy and see the world". But that holds true of all the three services of the Armed Forces.

Today, as the world is shrinking, there is a lot of interaction and as such the military personnel are constantly touring foreign countries for expositions or exercises, whether it is air shows, fleet reviews or peacekeeping missions. Many go on diplomatic postings or are sent for undergoing certain formal courses.

6. *Pay and Perks:* The pay scales in the Armed Forces are fairly competitive and in most cases, the perks include accommodation. The living quarters—the cantonment areas or the designated townships—invariably have good surroundings and are ordered. The officers are the cream of society, and they have an unmistakably enhanced quality of life.

Contrary to some notions, the Armed Force personnel are not war-mongers; they are simply conscientious soldiers carrying out the duty of defending their nation against external threats. But there are facets to their work which many of us do not know. A career in the Armed Forces makes for a wholesome personality, and indeed, a wholesome life.

❑

4

ADOLESCENCE AND PUBERTY

Growing Pains: When people talk about puberty, teenagers and adolescence, the things that come to mind are: raging hormones, cracking voices, budding breasts, menstruation, cranky, rebellious teenagers, sprouting hair, acne, wearing brass for the first time, and razor knicks on fresh-faced youth.

The onset of puberty is the most obvious sign of 'growing up' physically. To put it more formally, puberty can be defined as "a biological or physiological process characterised by the maturation of the sexual organs and the appearance of secondary sexual characteristics." People often think that puberty and adolescence refer to the same thing.

However, they refer to two different aspects of growing up. While puberty covers the physical, adolescence deals with the mental and has been described as a "psycho-social process characterised by mental and social growth, and often extending from puberty to the early 20s and sometimes beyond."

A Question of Hormones: When does this transformation begin? For girls it can happen any time between the ages of 8 and 12, while for boys it usually begins a couple of years later than girls. But there is no such thing as the right time. So there's no point wondering why she has breasts and you don't or why he's got a mustache and you don't.

So what exactly happens? It's as if a switch clicks on in the brain and activates a section of the brain called the hypothalamus. The hypothalamus, in turn, triggers the pituitary gland to produce two hormones—Follicle-Stimulating Hormone (FSH) and Luteinising Hormone (LH). The pituitary gland also releases a growth hormone called somatotropin.

FSH and LH are released cyclically in females and play a key role in the menstrual cycle. They stimulate the ovaries to secrete estrogen and progesterone and are responsible for the growth of the egg in the ovary. In the case of males, these hormones target the testes, which are responsible for the production of sperm and testosterone. The hypothalamus and pituitary gland monitor the level of testosterone in the blood and produce more or less releasing factors to raise and lower the testosterone levels as required.

First Brass and New Razors: While all this is happening on the inside, what's going on the outside? As a result of all this hormonal activity, girls' breasts get bigger and it's time to buy their first brass; they become more hairy, especially in the pubic area and they begin to menstruate. Boys, on the other hand, suddenly shoot up in height, downy fuzz appears on their chins and upper lips attempting to pass off as a beard and mustache; their voices crack at the most crucial and embarrassing moments; and finally, their penises and testes grow.

Emotional Roller Coaster: Most adolescents are uncomfortable and self-conscious about their growing breasts and suddenly awkward limbs. They feel that people are looking at them differently. Every pimple seems magnified a hundred times and girls hunch over trying to conceal their growing bust lines. To make matters worse, most parents are at a loss when faced with their children's budding sexuality. They cannot accept the fact that their 'babies' are talking and thinking about sex. As a result, adolescents are ecstatic one minute, irritable and moody the next. On one hand, they display a newfound maturity in keeping with their 'adult' status. On the other, they throw tantrums that could rival a three-year-old.

Puberty and adolescence bring with them a lot of emotional baggage. People in their adolescent years feel like they are in a twilight zone, hanging somewhere in the middle of childhood and adulthood. It's as if they're sitting on an emotional seesaw, feeling 'up' one minute, down the next; feeling old on some days, and like a child on others. It is a difficult time, but it makes one feel better to think that everyone goes through it.

GENERATION GAP

My Child thinks I'm her Enemy: Parents, when their offspring enter the dreaded teen years, look back nostalgically on the days when their children hadn't learned to speak yet, were cute and adoring, and hung on to every word that their parents said. One day, puberty happens and the sweet angels of yesterday begin to act like their parents are their worst enemies.

Kamini Sundaram says, "I don't know what's come over my daughter, Padma. She's always arguing with me about the silliest things. A single day doesn't go by without her screaming at me and storming out of the room. I don't know how to deal with her. In my day, I was not allowed to raise my voice to my parents."

Jacob Abraham is as confused about his son, Vivek. He says, "I've always wanted to give my son the best of things, but his demands never seem to end. He's constantly asking me for money to go out to pubs and discos and to buy the 'latest' clothes. If I say no, he makes me feel like a tyrant and says that none of the other parents object."

Being 'grown up' isn't all Fun and Games: Teenagers are a mass of confusion as they sit on the fence between their childhood and adulthood. Growing up can be quite scary. While being 'grown up' has many attractions, the responsibilities that go with it often come as a nasty surprise. For instance, teenagers want to stay out till all hours of the night, but when it comes to waking up in the morning in time for classes, it's a different story. Parents must make them understand that if they want to party hard, they must also work hard.

My Child is Ashamed of Me: Parents may feel a little like discarded old shoes, as friends become all-important to their children. It's not unusual for teenagers to go through a phase when they feel ashamed of their parents, afraid that their might not live up to their friends' standards. This can be very hurtful for parents, but they shouldn't take it personally. Just be cordial to your children's friends and maintain a distance. However, do not brook any discourteous behaviour for your children.

I Want My Freedom: Teenagers are always talking about their freedom, usually in context of how their parents are obstacles. The minute you give children a curfew, or object to their clothes or hair, or do not allow them to go away for the weekend, you become the evil dictator who will never understand. Suddenly, 'generation gap' becomes a buzzword. It's as if one day you and your child find yourselves on opposite sides of the fence and there's no meeting ground. Each one feels that the other is speaking a foreign language.

Age is More than a Number: However, parents don't realise that if they were to throw in the towel and let their teenagers run wild without any supervision, it would be a truly frightening experience for their children. Teenagers may not know it or admit it, but they need their parents to guide them about what's right and what's wrong. This is one area where age does matter and no matter how things change, parents should go with their instincts when it comes to deciding that some things are just not done.

Communication is the Key: This is the time when teenagers try to become individuals in their own right and try to move out from under the protective wing of their parents. They will try out many things in order to be 'in' with the crowd whether it's smoking, drinking, wearing skimpy clothes or even losing their virginity. This is not the time to play the great dictator and alienate your children. Talk to them, but don't talk down to them.

The way to do it, is not by making yourself out to be the enemy and coming down on them heavily for every transgression (and there will be many). Try to lay down the ground rules right in the beginning. It is difficult for anyone to interpret the teenage mind, but try to convey the fact that you're on their side. Parents tend to forget that they were teenagers too once and their self-righteousness doesn't win them any points with their children. Most parents tend to forget that babies do grow up someday and when the time comes, they must let them go and find their own way in the world. You can't protect your children forever and they won't thank you if you try to.

TEENS' BEHAVIOUR

Is your teenager rude? Often parents ignore this rudeness, believing it to be normal behaviour for teens. This is not true.

Not all teenagers are rude to their parents. Many of them are best friends with their mothers. Although occasional fights are normal, rudeness and rebellious behaviour needs to be checked at the earliest.

Check rudeness firmly the first time it happens. If your young child is rude to you, let him know in no uncertain terms, that this is simply not acceptable. Although you would love to be a friend to your child, such friendship does not include rudeness. Similarly, you too should avoid being rude to your child.

Check Insolence at Every Step: If one incident of rudeness slips by, your child will believe it is acceptable to speak in this manner. He then keeps pushing the boundaries, seeing how far you will take his cheek. Remember that your child is not deliberately trying to hurt you, but you may have unknowingly hurt him deeply when you denied something– even though it may be for his own good. This makes him want to lash out at you in the only way he can. If your child's desires are constantly ignored, it will be harder and harder for him to control his frustrations. Try being lenient with him in some matters, and intolerant of rudeness.

If rudeness is left unchecked when your child is young, it is likely to spiral when your child reaches her teens–so check insolence at every step.

Don't Underestimate Peer Influence: Peer pressure exerts its strongest influence on a teenager. At no stage in life is a person as vulnerable to the influences of his friends, as when he is in his teens. Support from friends is of prime importance. When you have a fight with your teen, she knows she can run to a friend and pour out her heart at being frustrated with your behaviour. Her friend will support her fully, and is likely to bring you down in the bargain.

Communicate with Your Teen: Other teenagers see their friends speaking to their parents rudely, and may try the same thing at home. It is important that you put a firm stop to it as soon as it begins. Try and do this without losing your temper or getting indignant at the way she just spoke to you. Ask her why she felt she needed to speak in such a rude manner. If you reason with your child and keep your cool, tempers need not be raised. Communication is very important. Always try and understand why she acts in a certain way, and what is going through her mind. And once you've clarified matters, be sure you let her know that no matter how angry she is, she cannot speak to you in a certain way.

Let her realise that different families are different, and you are very different from her friends' parents. What is scary is some friends may really speak poorly about their parents for whatever reason, and your child could then get tempted to join in with her inputs! And when she finds this support with friends, she gets bolder at home. This boldness first shows itself in rudeness and then defiance for your authority.

PEER PRESSURE

Vidya Bhagwat was horrified when she caught her teenage son trying to creep into the house in an obviously inebriated condition at three in the morning. She recounts, "I was shocked to see my 14-year-old son reeking of alcohol and barely able to stand on his feet. I could see that there was no point talking to him right then, but I didn't spare him the next day. His excuse was that all his friends were drinking and he didn't want to be a prude. And then to make things worse, he actually began to argue saying that it wasn't a 'big deal' anyway and that he knew I wouldn't understand."

Sumit Roy found a packet of cigarettes in his 16-year-old son's backpack. He says, "I just didn't know how to react. I confronted Amish and he had the audacity to tell me that I couldn't say anything to him, as I was a smoker myself. Besides, most of his friends smoked. He said it was just a 'social thing' and that they just smoked a few cigarettes at parties. I'm just worried that today it's nicotine, but tomorrow it could be marijuana or something worse. If I tell him that, he just tells me to relax. I can see I'm not getting through to him."

These are situations every parent has to face at some point. If it's not drinking, it's smoking or inappropriate dressing or late nights or overspending...the list is endless and so are the arguments. There seems to be no solution as parents and teenagers talk themselves hoarse trying to explain their respective points of view, their arguments apparently falling on deaf ears.

Parents, speaking as adults who have forgotten the angst of their teenage years tend to discount the very real power of peer pressure. For teenagers, desperately trying to fit in, peer pressure is something that they find very difficult to withstand. However, conscientious parents are not going to allow their children to blindly live by the dictates of their peer group if it's not good for them. This is the age when children are trying to find themselves and develop their value systems. At this time, it is their parents and not their peers who will be their best guides. Unfortunately, they can't see that.

The question is how do parents counteract the effects of peer pressure? Most of them follow the traditional method of criticism and condemnation that increases in frequency with every transgression till it becomes plain nagging. Even as adults we know how effective that is. It isn't. Your teenager will simply tune you out. They will feel that you never have anything good to say so why bother listening. This is definitely not the response you want to get. Here are some tips that should help you become more adept at counteracting the forces of peer pressure.

Tips for dealing with peer pressure:

- Do not take peer pressure lightly. Your teenager is at a time in his life when he doesn't know whether he is an adult or a child. Suddenly everybody's expectations seem to change. Nothing seems to be constant or predictable. He is trying to spread his wings, but is still scared to let go. In this time of confusion, the only people he feels he can identify with and who will empathise are his peers. He is desperate to belong as he seeks his identity.
- Your teenager is going to do many things that you don't agree with or approve of. However, if you make an issue of everything, he will just think that you're picking on him. What you need to do is turn a blind eye on the pierced bellybutton and the outlandish

clothes. Concentrate on adhering strictly to curfews imposed on him and other serious issues like smoking, drinking, drug abuse, sex, etc. In this way, you maintain your credibility with him and he may even be more willing to listen because you haven't had a fit because he dyed his hair blue.

- Adopt a democratic rather than an autocratic approach. If you are going to impose any rules, first talk to your teenager. See what he expects and try to reach some kind of middle ground when laying down the law. In this way, your teenager is a little more likely to toe the line as he himself has participated in drawing it.
- However, once the both of you have decided on the limits, they should be treated as if they were written in stone. Well, maybe not as inflexible as that, but he doesn't have to know that. Set your limits very clearly so that there's no room for argument and also specify the consequences of any transgressions. Once the ground rules have been laid, enforce them strictly so that they have some meaning.
- Remember that teenagers are human after all, and may be a little more fallible than most at this stage of their lives. There are bound to be times when peer pressure will rule. At such times, your teenager should feel that he could talk to you about it, expecting that you will understand, rather than doing things behind your back and maybe worsening the situation. To put it more simply, he should know that he can come to you when he is in a jam and even though you may give him the firing of a lifetime, ultimately you are on his side.
- Identify another teenager with a good sense of values in your child's social circle and subtly encourage their friendship. After all, two is always better than one when it comes to withstanding peer pressure.

- Point out role models in real life and in books and films who have dared to be different and achieved something.
- At this stage your teenager is very unsure about the way he looks, about what people think of him, and about where his life is going in general. He is not going to think of you as a friend if you constantly criticise and berate him. Take the trouble to praise him for his accomplishments or just for being 'good.' This will make him feel that you too are on his side and his peer group will have less of a hold on him.

DRUG AND ALCOHOL MENACE

Teenagers are Bound to Experiment: It's a fact of life that teenagers are likely to experiment with sex, drugs, alcohol, clothes and make-up on the fast track to adulthood. The question is what are you, as a parent going to do about it? While all parents will agree that something must be done, they're not sure what exactly to do.

The problem that most parents face is that they just cannot accept the fact that their 'babies' are smoking, drinking, indulging in heavy petting, or worse, even 'going all the way.' They have just one thought in their minds that children this age should not be doing these things. Beyond that, they seem to become incapable of thought and action. They just want to bury their heads in the sand and hope that the problem will sort itself out. At a loss for words, parents often unknowingly build an invisible wall between themselves and their teenage children. And this is exactly what a parent should never do.

The Dictatorial Approach: At times like this, playing the great dictator can backfire. Using words like, "because I said so" as the only explanation is bound to encourage defiance. You will have to come down from your "I'm older so I know best" pedestal and talk to your teenager in a language that he can understand. You have to communicate to him that you are both on the same side and that you sympathise with his need to be 'cool' and be one of the gang, but at the same time you are concerned about him.

Lectures are a surefire turn-off for the average teenager. After all, it is not like they think smoking and drinking is good for health. And the fact that they do it behind their parents' backs just shows that they are well aware that parental approval for smoking dope and drinking beer is not forthcoming.

Why Drugs and Alcohol? There are several reasons why a teenager may take drugs or alcohol. Some teenagers are just bored and like to experiment, while others do it to be accepted by their peers. Teenagers who are shy, lonely and lack self-confidence often find that drugs and alcohol transform them into life of the party. For them, these vices are the key to social success. When they are 'high', teenagers find that they are more assertive and their troubles seem far away and unimportant. They take drugs and alcohol to escape from family problems or to relieve the tension of performing well academically and otherwise. In the ultimate analysis, it is the 'kick' or the 'buzz' that they get that makes them go back for more.

What You can do About It? The first thing that parents should do is to bring up their children with good values. If children are confident, feel that they can trust their own judgement and are taught that it's all right to do their own thing, it will make them more resistant to peer pressure. Parents should convey to their children that they shouldn't be afraid to say 'no.'

Parents should set an example by not drinking excessively and cutting down on their smoking. They should serve non-alcoholic beverages at their parties in addition to alcohol. They should not encourage their children to take sips from their drinks.

It may help to talk about drugs and alcohol in a general way to avoid putting your teenager on the defensive. You can talk about someone who has a drug problem or the time when your colleague misbehaved at the office party because he had too much to drink. The minute you act like sex, drugs and alcohol are taboo subjects, you are cutting your child loose in the big, bad world. Parents need to be well informed about the kind of drugs that a teenager is likely to have access to and be aware whether alcohol is the norm on social occasions.

If you suspect that your teenager is smoking or hitting the bottle, there's no point coming down on him like a sledgehammer. Get to the root of the problem. You need to talk to him about why he feels he the need to smoke and drink, despite being aware of the consequences. You should try to keep an open mind when talking to your teenager. Make an effort to remember your own rebellious phase as a teenager (don't say that you didn't have one). While you may not agree with your teenager's way of establishing his independence, the feeling is the same.

When you adopt an open attitude, you are also keeping the lines of communication open. Thus, your teenager will not hesitate to come to you for advice or just to talk. Try not to be judgemental and disapproving. It really doesn't help. If your child develops a serious addiction, be prepared for denial, defiance and irrational behaviour. You should seek professional help, but remember that your child will not respond unless he feels ready to be helped.

Adolescence is a period of contradiction for teenagers. While they want to spread their wings, they also want their parents to guide them, though they would never admit it. Parents should take heart from the fact that even though their teenage children might act like know-it-alls, they crave parental guidance as they stumble and fumble through new experiences.

SOCIAL GRACES

Social graces bring confidence. Often children are unsure as to how to behave in a particular social situation, and this makes them uneasy, causing them to lose confidence. Kids can get away with running around the place, but teenagers tend to feel awkward. They frequently wait for a cue from their parents as to how to behave, and if that cue doesn't come, they waver around uncertainly, not sure what to do next. Make sure you instill certain graces in your child, so he doesn't have to wait for that cue.

Mallika, a teenager I know, went up to Vikas, another teenager she had met once before, and said hello. Instead of responding in kind, he looked at her blankly and said 'Er... who are you?' She re-introduced herself, spoke for a minute and walked on, but not without feeling slightly insulted.

Teach your son that if someone he does not recognise comes up and says hi, instead of cheekily declaring 'who are you?' he should smile back in acknowledgement, and try and figure out who the person is during the conversation. Or he could politely state, "You look so familiar, but I just cannot seem to place you." The same rule, of course, does not apply to teenage girls, who are often approached by random boys. In any case, being polite has never hurt anyone.

Your friends drop in for a cup of tea when your children are lounging around watching MTV. Make sure they stand up and greet the guests. A causal wave or nod of acknowledgement is not enough, unless, of course, the guest is practically a family member. Even so, practice makes perfect, and the more often your child gets up to greet guests, the more naturally and easier it will come to him.

If you are out for dinner at a restaurant, and are waiting for guests to join you, your children, along with the father, should stand up as the guests approach your table. The lady may remain seated.

TABLE MANNERS

If guests come over and your children are in their room, it is always nice if they can come out and say hi. If they are not suitably attired and are loath to change their clothes, you could excuse them, but if it is a family member who would be pleased to meet the kids, they should definitely come out and greet them.

If guests stop by when you are not at home, your teenager should invite them in, offer them something to drink and sit with them until they leave. (Only if your teenager knows who they are. It is understandable if your teenager doesn't invite strangers when he or she is alone at home. It is important for them to use their discretion here. Younger children should never answer the door.)

Teach your children to offer to carry anything heavy and weighty, and to help you carry stuff to and fro. This does not mean that you sound them off for not offering to carry that light-as-a-feather plastic bag. They are not coolies. There is nothing more annoying than mothers goading their children on to 'help' a relative carry something no heavier than an envelope, just so she can feel proud to have such thoughtful children. But if you or any elder is carrying an assortment of packages, or something weighty or uncomfortable, your child should rush forward to help.

Teach Your Son To:

- Open the entrance door for women
- Open the car door for women
- Stand aside and wait for women to exit the elevator before he does
- Wait for the ladies to sit down first
- Stand up when being introduced
- Apologise for swearing in front of elders or women

And most importantly, teach your teenagers to be friendly. It is not 'cool' to be standoffish. It is far cooler to be a well-mannered, confident and warm person.

EXPOSURE TO THE WORLD

Although you may have lived with your parents until your marriage, do not assume your children will do the same.

In India, most daughters continue living at home until they get married. However, this is changing, and now we see more and more young girls striking out on their own, to make a life for themselves.

Parents in India often try and ensure that their daughters lead a very sheltered life until their marriage. Then the responsibility of caring for their daughter passes on to her husband and his family.

Children Move Out: But more and more children now move out of their parents' homes either to study in different towns, or to work elsewhere.

They have No Exposure: What happens then is these girls often don't know what to expect, and are unprepared for many situations that may arise. 21-year-old Rima was so sheltered her entire life, that when she got her first job in an advertising firm, she suffered a culture shock. She had never been exposed to women that smoked, and when suddenly she found herself in an office filled with women who constantly held a burning cigarette between their fingers, it disturbed her greatly, and she felt very uncomfortable in their presence, believing she would never fit in. She did, over time, without picking up the habit herself. It helped that she was still living at home, surrounded by her parents and loving siblings, with who she could discuss the events of the day and her feelings.

On the other hand, if she had been exposed to something so radically different from her present lifestyle when she was no longer living at home, she may have taken up smoking herself either with a desire to fit in or simply to try something that seemed new and exiting.

What helped was that Rima, although sheltered earlier on, was given an exposure to life outside her shell, when still living with her parents.

Don't Shelter them too Much: As a parent should try and expose your child to as much as you can and as you believe feasible, while they are still living with you. Naturally this doesn't mean that you introduce them to drugs or smoking, but you do need to encourage them to go out more with their friends instead of curtailing their socialising. This way they will be exposed to many more things at an age when they are still living with you, and you can help them make the right choices. If they are exposed to these things when they are no longer with you, you will not be around to guide them towards the right path.

Encourage Socialising: Parents in India often shudder at the thought of sending their daughter to a nightclub. Before denying permission, think about the fact that although she may never go to one when she is living with you, she will when she is no longer with you. It may make more sense to let her go now, and ensure she reaches home early. Exposure in little doses is far better than none at all, or sudden exposure.

IMPORTANT TIPS

Teenagers often make the wrong choices because of lack of knowledge. Here's what you should let them know about the two evils: smoking and drinking.

Smoking: Often, teenagers pick up smoking in the company of their friends. If your child's friends smoke, it is likely that your child will pick it up as well. Remember that if your child smokes, don't think of it as the end of the world. Many parents are devastated when they get to know that their child smokes. Understand that there will be a time when, a few years down the line, your child will himself want to quit. Pushing and punishing him will only delay the process. The best thing is to explain the dangers of smoking to your child at the outset.

Smoking kills, and second-hand smoke is just as dangerous so you need to set an example at home. If you smoke, never smoke inside the home because you are endangering the health of your family. This is why smoking indoors in public places– including pubs–is banned in many parts of the world. Teenagers also mistakenly believe that it is okay to smoke light cigarettes. They realise that smoking is bad for their health; no one wants to get addicted.

So they believe that if they smoke light cigarettes as opposed to regular or strong ones, they are less likely to get addicted. They also believe that light cigarettes contain less nicotine, less tobacco and less tar than regular cigarettes. This belief is wrong. Light cigarettes contain fewer chemicals that give you a head rush, but more of other chemicals, and are equally dangerous, if not more so, for your health in other ways.

Teenagers don't know this, which is why more than 50 per cent of teenagers who smoke, opt for light cigarettes. Similarly, later on if a person wants to quit smoking, he believes that switching to lighter cigarettes is a step closer to quitting. Not true. So the next time you explain the dangers of smoking to your child, make sure you let him know that it is just as dangerous to smoke light cigarettes.

Alcohol: Many youngsters go through a stage of partying or wanting to party, drinking and vomiting. It is almost like a rite of passage. Before you start getting sleepless nights over this, remember that it is far better that your child can confide in you than spends the night out with his friends to hide from you the fact that he had a little too much to drink. Yes, you can lecture to your child about the dangers of drinking too much, but once your child vomits, chances are that he will be far more careful about the amount he has to drink the next time. This is how your child learns his limits.

Don't encourage your child to start drinking, but if he does, don't stop him from doing so either, because he will just continue to do so, but behind your back. In fact, it is far better to explain to your child that he should drink within his limits, and be firm about sticking to his limits. Also, many children believe that drinking is a fun thing to do, but there is something known as alcohol poisoning, and if a person has far too much to drink at one go, he may need to be hospitalised to pump out the alcohol or it can be fatal.

PROBLEM TEENS

Is your teen giving you problems? At times such problems escalate seemingly to the point of no return. Here's help.

Managing teenagers is a full-time job for some parents as they turn themselves into 24-hour police to monitor the consequences doled out for misdeeds. You constantly keep trying to figure out what your teen is up to, while your teenager keeps trying to hide his life from you. So, a game of cat and mouse develops and as the game continues, your child starts getting bolder and bolder, while the parent starts applying more restrictions to their child's life, and coming up with harsher punishments.

The net result is that resentment builds and while some teens even go to the extent of running away from home, most teens turn defiant, rebellious, start lying to their parents, and turn to alcohol, drugs and smoking as a means of escape. Long gone is the kind and loving relationship of earlier years.

When the relationship is spiralling out of control and parents find themselves at their wits end, the challenge is to try and placate your child, and see if you can build your relationship from scratch. Harsher, more restrictive consequences will not bring your teen "under control". Slowly and deliberately trying to 'woo' your teen can rekindle the relationship you feel you have almost lost.

Step by Step: As a parent, you should make the first step in going out of your way to find moments when they can approach your teen by showing an interest in their activities or to provide a positive comment. For instance, if your teen is seated at the computer, approach, place a hand gently on his shoulder and ask what he is doing. Then nod, as if interested, make a neutral comment such as "oh", or "aha"... and then walk away.

Thus, slowly start rebuilding your relationship. When you are already at a stage of sour relationship with your child, trying to push yourself on your child too hard will only worsen the situation. You too need to 'play it cool' initially, and earn your child's trust. Take slow steps to start rekindling rapport with your teen. On other occasions, perhaps when chauffeuring your teen here and there, make a stop such as at a dosa or burger joint, and offer to grab a couple of burgers or idlis. This will help the two of you to have some fun together, and is a step in a right direction. Use time with your teen constructively, to gain an insight into her life, and not to lecture her with what she is doing wrong.

Guide: Most parents lose sight of the fact that they need to guide their children and not control them. Try and restrict your controlling impulses and guide your child by getting his feedback, and by trying to meet your child's demands halfway when giving permission for certain activities.

Arguments: Throughout, step away from escalating any arguments. Alternately, when your teen acts inappropriately, quietly and directly express your disapproval and then walk away. You want to leave the teen thinking about their behaviour, not yours. While you cannot control your teen's behaviour, you can control your own.

Issues: If there are serious concerns related to school attendance, drugs or alcohol, try to discuss your concerns and if this isn't possible, make an appointment with the school counsellor to address these or other issues. Demonstrate to your teen that you will use appropriate strategies with their well-being in mind as opposed to them feeling you are just trying to exert your will or control over them through "discipline". Don't push them too hard and then try to make them understand that it is all for their own good. Make sure that your actions show you are trying to act for their own good.

If your child is violent, tell them that rather than engaging in counter-violence, you will call the police, and do so if need be! Your child should know that certain kinds of behaviour will not be accepted. It is not that your teen should avoid the consequences of their behaviour, but that you should engage them in ways that can promote the relationship and your influence. This is how you can reduce any conflicts you have with your teen, build rapport, continue to hold them accountable and help them develop appropriate life skills. It starts with you as a parent, taking responsibility as the grown-up to foster the relationship. While you may not believe it will work, you know the other way didn't. Take the leap of faith and try.

CAUSE OF DEPRESSION

Adolescence is a stage of life when teenagers go through a period of uncertainty and confusion as they try to find their feet and establish their independence. Everything seems in a state of flux—their moods, their bodies, and their relationships with family and friends. They are painfully conscious of their maturing bodies. They feel socially inept. They swing wildly between being shy and embarrassed to brash and rebellious in a bid to disguise their insecurities and confusion. Most teenagers emerge unscathed or maybe with just a few nicks and bruises. But there are others who just cannot cope with the tumult of emotions and they fall into a depression.

Depression is an all-encompassing gloom that envelops every aspect of a person's existence. It is different from the sadness one feels when one thinks of a rift within the family or the unhappiness associated with the failure to get into the university of your choice. Depression is not a mood or a phase. A depressed person feels that there is something fundamentally wrong with him and his life. He feels incapable of handling the smallest problems. He feels that nothing ever goes his way and that may be he doesn't deserve to be happy.

SIGNS OF DEPRESSION

Defeatist Attitude: Depressed teenagers feel that they are destined to fail at anything that they attempt. They take failure personally seeing it as being directly related to their personalities rather than to anything they might have done. For instance, if they are snubbed at a party by an acquaintance, they will assume that it is because they are boring and not worth knowing. A normal teenager would just shrug it off and move on to the next person. As a result of this defeatist attitude, depressed teenagers rarely make the effort to do anything because they believe that they will fail anyway.

Impulsive Behaviour: Teenagers affected by depression also tend to act on impulse. They feel that since they have no control over their circumstances and cannot seem to find a solution to any of their problems, they should do something and then forget about it.

Socially Withdrawn: A depressed teenager is often withdrawn and anti-social because he feels that nobody would want him around. He feels that he has nothing of interest to say and does not have the necessary social skills to make him well-liked. He will avoid volunteering for any group activities assuming that he will be a burden and that he has nothing of value to contribute.

Uncomfortable Sharing Personal Information: Teenagers afflicted with depression are uncomfortable talking about themselves because they think that the listener will judge them and find them wanting in every way. They do not want to open themselves up to any possible disapproval or criticism, which they take for granted as being forthcoming.

Psychosomatic Illnesses: Depression can result in a teenager displaying psychosomatic symptoms like dizzy spells, headaches, stomachaches, etc. in an attempt to garner some sympathy. They feel that this is the only way they can get some positive attention. Their supposed indisposition can also get them out of uncomfortable situations that they may not want to face.

Wants to be Someone Else: A teenager is usually depressed because he doesn't like the person he is. He attributes all his problems to some basic flaw in his personality. Often he looks at his peers, especially the popular ones, and wishes he looked like them or had their money or their intelligence, which would guarantee that people would like him and find him interesting.

OVERCOMING DEPRESSION

- The first thing to do is to help your teenager set realistic short-term goals. Ask him for suggestions on how he would like to improve his life? Then help him identify some simple steps he can take to achieve these goals. Remember not to set goals, which are unattainable, as this will just reinforce his belief that he is a failure. On the other hand, do not aim for things that are easily attainable. The whole idea is that your teenager must feel that he has been equal to the challenge.
- Make sure that you encourage him at every step and help him in every way possible without actually doing his work for him. For instance, if he wants to audition for a play, help him rehearse and boost his confidence without giving him false hope.
- If he fails to reach his set goals, do not try to sweep it under the carpet and smooth it over with inanities like "you'll do better next time." Acknowledge his failure and discuss why it happened. Maybe he gave up too easily or didn't study hard enough or had a panic attack. It's important to get this out in the open so that you know what your teenager attributes his

failure to and correct any misconceptions that he may have.

- Do not compare your teenager to his peers and find him wanting. Don't say things like "why can't you be like that?" You will just be reinforcing his belief that he's not good enough the way he is, even for you. You have to teach him that he can admire others without necessarily envying them. If he comments in an envious tone about another teenager's attributes, admit that the other child is good, but point out something that your teenager is good at.
- Depressed teenagers tend to vacillate over every decision. This is because they don't trust their own judgement and need to be constantly reassured that they are doing the 'right thing.' You have to help your teenager make decisions in a way that he will learn to trust his own judgement. It is also important that you insist that once he has made a choice, he must go through with it and cope with the consequences, whatever they are.
- Short-term measures like buying your teenager tickets to a concert or taking him for a holiday are not going to alleviate his depression. You are going to have to sit down and talk to him about what exactly it is that bothers him and how he can overcome it. You have to take steps to make him feel empowered so that he feels that he can effectively accomplish the things he sets out to do.

NEXT GENERATION AND FUTURE

It's a tough, crazily competitive world out there, and it seems to have everyone tense and worried—about coping, about getting ahead in life, about keeping up with the Joneses. And these standard stress triggers appear to be even more acute in the case of those balancing the tightrope teen years.

How do those making the precarious transition from childhood to adulthood, from school to college and the big, bad world outside cope with their growing pains? What are their fears, their aspirations? What is their view of the world outside? An opinion poll conducted among young persons in the age group of 15 to 20 in eight metropolitan cities (New Delhi, Mumbai, Chennai, Kolkata, Bangalore, Ahmedabad, Lucknow and Patna) tried to find a few answers.

Seventy-five per cent of the youngsters claimed that the teenage years were a time of stress and anxiety for them—anxiety about exams, jobs, parental expectations, peer pressure, love lives, the need to look good and dress smartly, and well, even the state of the nation.

Anxiety about performance in school or college and future job prospects seemed to affect more youngsters in Delhi than anywhere else, perhaps because competitive pressures are the greatest in the capital city. However, parental expectations seemed to be a source of anxiety to youngsters particularly in Ahmedabad and Chennai, maybe because traditional values have a stronger hold on these cities than elsewhere.

How do teenagers cope with pressures and anxieties? A larger percentage (36 per cent) said they turned to friends for help and advice rather than parents (30 per cent said they turned to the latter). However, it would appear that family relationships remain strong, in that 43 per cent (as against 39 per cent) asserted that there was no 'generation gap' in their family and that they felt comfortable sharing their problems with parents and siblings. Fifty-five per cent of the respondents, boys and girls equally, said they were closer to their mother than their father. A minority (45 per cent) asserted that religion was a source of strength for them in tackling personal problems. More boys than girls (28 per cent as against 13 per cent) and more college-goers than school-goers (24 per cent as against 16 per cent) had had sex; and most did not view it as a problem, but as a solution! Only a small minority said they smoked (25 per cent) or drank liquor (18 per cent), but more boys than girls and more college students than school students had these habits. Surprisingly, however, more school students (10 per cent) than college students (7 per cent) said they had taken or tried drugs.

Despite all the pressures and anxieties they faced, a majority (about 57 per cent) said they were confident about their future and had sufficient freedom to achieve what they wanted. Surprisingly, there was no significant difference in the response of boys and girls in this respect. The respondents in Delhi, Chennai and Bangalore showed a significantly higher level of confidence in themselves than those in other cities. Confidence levels were lowest in Lucknow and Kolkata. Given a chance, would our youngsters prefer to go abroad? In this age of globalisation their sights seemed to be set far, and as many as 53 per cent (boys and girls equally) said yes, they would.

A cross-tabulation of the results brought out some interesting findings. The youngsters who said they had sufficient freedom and control over their lives were the ones more anxious about their academic performance, future prospects, lifestyle and family problems. This suggests that their anxiety actually has to do with their high aspiration levels and strong motivation. On the other hand, those who said they did not have sufficient freedom were the ones who also felt there was a generation gap in their families; they are more likely to be the ones who turn to smoking, liquor and drugs. The findings of the poll are subject to a sampling error of plus or minus 4 per cent.

❑

5

PSYCHOLOGICAL FACTORS

Introduction to screening young children for development and behaviour problems in primary care, emphasising standardised tools.

LEARNING OBJECTIVES

Impact of screening

Screening versus referral

Under-referral in screening

Know specific screening instruments

Screening young children for developmental, behavioural, and emotional problems is an important responsibility for paediatricians. This module provides information about screening techniques which can be used effectively and efficiently in the office setting. We provide background information on screening, and an annotated list of Developmental and Behavioural/Emotional screening tools.

THE OVERVIEW

About 16 per cent of children have disabilities such as speech-language impairments, mental retardation, learning disabilities, and emotional/behavioural disturbance. Although such children are twice as likely to seek health care as children without disabilities, only 20 per cent to

30 per cent of these children are detected prior to school entrance. The reasons are understandable: Many disabilities are subtle and children who have them may appear to be developing normally especially at younger ages.

Under-detection is nevertheless unfortunate because it may delay the possibilities of early intervention. Children who participate in early intervention programmes prior to kindergarten are more likely to graduate from high school, hold jobs, live independently, avoid teen pregnancy, delinquency and violent crime.

These positive outcomes save society between $30,000 and $100,000 per child. Put another way, for every $1,00, we spend on early intervention, society saves $7,00 - a savings so substantials that countries like England instituted the Sure Start Programme and offer a quality of early preschool programme to all low-income children.

Policy Statements: The American Academy of Pediatrics recognises these benefits. In the 2001 Policy Statement (Developmental Screening and Surveillance) from the AAP states:

> *"All infants and young children should be screened for developmental delays. Screening procedures should be incorporated into the ongoing health care of the child as part of the provision of a medical home, as defined by the Academy." The AAP also recommended that paediatricians "acquire skills in the administration and interpretation of reliable and valid developmental screening techniques appropriate for the population." In the AAP Statement both developmental surveillance and screening are mentioned as methods of early detection of disabilty.*

The American Academy of Neurology, in its Practise Parameter on diagnosis of autism (2000), stated:

> *"Developmental surveillance should be performed at all well-child visits from infancy through school-age, and at any age thereafter if concerns are raised about social acceptance, learning, or behaviour."*

Both of the AAP Statement and the AAN statement include recommended screening tools, many of the measures mentioned are relatively new and rely on information from parents. The advantage of this approach is that parents can complete them at home or while they wait for appointments. Clinicians and/or office staff need only score and interpret the results; saving substantial amounts of professional time.

The articles on screening are meant to help child health providers improve their efforts in developmental screening. However readers are encouraged to refer to the original published policy statements. Also, the AAP periodically reviews and revises policy statements.

EIPSDT: The Early Intervention Periodic Screening, Diagnosis and Treatment benefit under Medicaid, also calls for screening at each well visit. There has been controversy about how this requirement should be implemented. For example, there are currently 28 states engaged in class action lawsuits against Medicaid in several cases for failing to deliver on the promise of early screening.

Three states have settled their suits by agreeing to ensure that providers administer standardised, validated screens: Tennessee, North Carolina, and Louisiana.

Despite the economic, social, legal, and developmental benefits of early screening with standardised measures and early intervention when indicated, insurers are not especially generous at reimbursing health care providers' in their efforts to ensure that children are detected and referred for needed intervention.

What is Medicaid doing about Screening?: Medicaid is tackling this issue and trying to ensure that in all states, the

96110 procedure code for developmental/behavioural screening, carries reimbursement apart from ten bundled well visit if quality instruments are deployed. Even so, it behooves clinicians to use measures that are accurate but also quick and inexpensive. Screening is a means to a more important end—which is getting families needed assistance including referrals, delivery of information to families, developmental promotion, and enrollment in early intervention. So, swift administration and scoring of screens frees times for follow-up, resource identification, patient education, etc.

Who should be Screened?: Screening is designed for the asymptomatic—for those thought to be developing normally. Children with obvious problems can simply be referred promptly for early intervention. There is broad agreement that there should be a systematic way of identifying children who need to be evaluated for disabilty. There is a good evidence to support the use of a standardised, validated tools to do this screening. If only asymptomatic children are screened, children who might have been identified with screening may be missed.

Screening Tools: The AAP Developmental and Behavioural Screening statements lists a number of recommended screening tools. All improve existing detection rates by 3 to 4 times and will detect correctly almost all children with and without problems when used longitudinally. Tests included in the discussion are those with national standardisation, proven reliability, validation against a range of quality diagnostic measures, and sensitivity in the detection of children with problems and specificity in the detection of children without problems in keeping with standards for screening tests of at least 70 per cent to 80 per cent.

Issues in Screening via Information from Parents: Most parents can complete screens. However, many parents with limited education do not raise concerns spontaneously with health care providers. Such parents may not realise that developmental topics are a part of primary care. Thus, parent-report screens alert families that development is an important topic to providers and ensures that all parents have a voice in a pediatric encounter.

Even so, parents with limited education may have difficulty with literacy. Asking parents, in a sensitive manner, if they would prefer to have someone go through the measure with them should circumvent literacy barriers. Most screens are also published in languages such as Spanish, Vietnamese, French, etc., to help circumvent language barriers.

Some clinicians worry that highly educated parents are likely to be overly concerned about their children and that parent-report tools used with this group will result in over-referrals. Tests correct for this problem in various ways (e.g., by identifying those concerns not predictive of developmental or behavioural problems) so that clinicians can offer patient education instead of referrals. Even so, screens always produce some errors.

However, is important to know that over-referrals on screening tests (false-positives) tend to be on children who perform below average in the better predictors of school success, *i.e.*, intelligence, academics/pre-academics, and language skills, and to have numerous psychosocial risk factors. Identifying these children, even though they will not qualify for special education, can help providers link them with needed services such as Head Start, Early Head Start, after-school tutoring, summer school, quality day care and preschool, Boys and Girls' Clubs, parent training, etc.

PITFALLS OF SCREENING

Here are five major pitfalls of screening:

1. *Waiting until a Problem is Observable:* Clinicians often use screening tools only after they've noticed a problem. If the problem is obvious, referring is the

correct response. Screening such children may compound rather than reduce the error in both clinical judgment and screening tools because screening instruments are not intended for children with recognised problems.

2. *Ignoring Screening Results:* Many times, screening test results are not taken seriously and children who fail are not referred but rather viewed with a wait and see attitude. Good screens make a correct decision at least 70 per cent to 80 per cent of the time. Children over-referred by such screens tend to have numerous psychosocial risk factors and perform on diagnostic measures well below average. Thus over-referrals are children for whom extra attention from non-medical providers is invaluable. Children under-detected by screens at one visit are likely to be identified at a subsequent visit. Reliability studies conducted as a part of constructing quality screening measures ensure that the results will be virtually identical on a second administration. Thus, there is no evidence to support "temporising" in such a situation, and harm could result from delayed diagnosis and intervention.
3. *Relying on Informal Methods:* Informal tools such as checklists often contain items sure to miss most kids with problems (such as the checklists on many encounter forms). These are often based on instruments such as the original Denver Developmental Screening Test, that missed up to 50 per cent of mental retardation and 70 per cent of language impairment.

   Checklists provide no validated criteria for referral, and have unknown reliability. Remember, most developmental and behavioural problems are not obvious. Children usually walk although some do not walk well. They talk but may not talk well; read but not well. Discriminating between adequately developed and problematic levels of skills requires careful measurement. Validated and standardised tools carry the burden of proof that informal measures lack. We would never select tools for blood lead or other medical screens with questionable or unknown levels of accuracy. Why do we do this with development?

4. *Using a Measure not Suitable for Primary Care:* Most practises retain copies of tests such as the Denver-II or Gessell. Concerns about the accuracy of both measures aside, these tests also take longer to administer than the average length of a well visit. This results in two things: (1) using tests only with selected patients, usually those with observable problems; and (2) nonstandard administrations, such as administration of key items on the Denver-II. The former situation ignores the asymptomatic who are those most in need of screening while the latter reduces screens to the status of checklists with their inherent lack of criteria and unproven sensitivity and specificity.
5. *Assuming Services are Limited or Nonexistent:* Although the early childhood community has not always reached out to medical providers, services of good quality exist in every state for any child with developmental delays. It is a good idea to meet the local coordinators responsible for implementing child-find and intervention programmes under the Individuals with Disabilities with Education Act (IDEA). Encourage them to keep you posted on referrals and consider taking time to visit some programmes.

For information on programmes, the National Early Childhood Technical Assistance Centre has a website with contact information for every state and usually region for children 0-3 or 3-5 years. For children 5 years and older, contact a school psychologist in the child's school of zone or your local school board. Generally, IDEA programmes are a one stop shop and can provide not only broad early intervention and special education programmes but also many related services including mental health, physical, occupational, and speech therapies, parent training, etc.

It is also important to monitor the development of children who do not qualify for IDEA programmes but who still have developmental needs. Most of these children can be well served by a quality day care programme. When parents have limited income, children may be eligible for services through Head Start, Early Head Start or Migrant Worker Head Start.

There is a broad consensus that early identification of disability is both feasible and important. Improving the effectiveness of developmental screening and surveillance has the potential for improving the lives of countless children and families. There is also good evidence that more effective identification will result in cost savings to society.

SCHOOL READINESS

Parents and Professionals Speak on Social and Emotional Needs of Young Children: The first national goal for education, that "by the year 2000, all children in America will start school ready to learn," reflects a belief that achievements in the earliest years of life are fundamental to later school-based learning and academic success. Although the definition and assessment of school readiness has been interpreted in many different ways (Kagan, 1990), there is widespread concern that increasing numbers of children begin formal schooling without the requisite skills or abilities to succeed. According to a Carnegie survey of over 7,000 kindergarten teachers, 35 per cent of this country's children are not ready for academic work when they begin school. When asked what most restricted school readiness, the teachers cited deficiencies in language and emotional maturity.

This study is an assessment of the hazards and fuelling stations on the road toward school readiness as viewed by parents and child development professionals in two socio-economically disadvantaged communities. Taken singly and in combination, socio-economic factors such as poverty, lack of parental education, teen and single-parenthood are well-recognised risk factors for school difficulty (Centre for the Study of Social Policy, The Annie E. Casey Foundation, 1993).

However, this study was not designed to define the socio-economic status or service utilisation of the participating sites, nor are the samples necessarily representative of the broader geographic communities. Rather, the goal was to identify potential precursors to later kindergarten difficulties that would suggest specific areas needing further study and support. The framework and methodology were guided by several assumptions of experts in the field of infant and toddler development.

Assumption 1: Children are Born "Ready to Learn"

Extraordinary first lessons result from ordinary everyday events between adults and young children. In a caring environment, children's relationships with adults teach them to feel effective, important, and safe. Because early experiences affect the various developmental domains separately and in combination, seemingly simple activities—such as play with a warm and responsive caregiver—can promote a wide range of abilities, including problem-solving skills, language development, and emotion regulation.

In contrast, inconsistent and insensitive parenting inhibits natural curiosity and ambition; as a consequence, children can grow to feel helpless and wary of new opportunities for learning. The first years of life are also fundamental to children's ability to behave in socially acceptable ways. Parents' behaviours and beliefs about appropriate ways to express emotion, resolve conflict, persuade, and cooperate with others have a profound influence on toddlers' abilities to get along with peers, follow rules, cooperate with adults, and ultimately, to become useful and caring citizens.

By age three, competent children are those who are: self- confident and trusting, intellectually inquisitive, able to use language to communicate, physically and mentally healthy, able to relate well toward others, and empathic toward others (Carnegie Task Force on Meeting the Needs of Young Children, 1994). These accomplishments, impressive in their own right, continue to be important because they determine how well a child will navigate subsequent developmental tasks—including the transition to formal schooling.

Assumption 2: School Readiness is a Cumulative Construct

Readiness depends on multiple prior experiences and achievements. One source of individual variation in readiness reflects the outcome of stage-salient tasks of earlier developmental periods. For example, longitudinal studies begun in infancy find that secure infant-parent attachment at one year of age is associated with greater self-confidence and self-motivated learning in the toddler years (e.g., Sroufe, 1979). Given the continuity in developmental competence over the first years of life, there are strong theoretical and empirical reasons to believe that precursors to some later school difficulties can be identified and ameliorated well before school entry.

Assumption 3: The Quality of Early Learning Experiences and Parent-child Interaction Depend on Multiple, Interdependent Economic, Psychologic, and Social Influences

Such influences include families' personal and economic resources, parents' knowledge and beliefs regarding children's development, formal and informal support systems, and public policies and practises that impinge on work and family life. For example, as a result of changes in the American economy and family structure, more parents are struggling to balance home and work responsibilities, often with fewer financial, community, and familial supports than those of previous generations. Housing, transportation, health care, and childcare all cost proportionately more than in the past, and the value of minimum wage has declined.

In addition to these financial burdens, today's parents move more often to keep pace with housing and job opportunities. As a result, families seem more isolated. They are less likely to live near older, trusted family members who traditionally helped young people prepare for parenthood and shared the responsibility for childrearing. Fear of neighbourhoods crime and violence increases social isolation further by limiting the number of safe places for children to play and limiting opportunities for parents to build new supportive friendships.

Assumption 4: Families have Primary Responsibility for raising Competent and Caring Children

There are many ways in which communities, including neighbours, educators, law enforcement agents, social service, and health service providers, can help families raise competent and caring children. However, successful strategies—including those that promote school readiness and school success—depend on the needs and priorities that families identify for their children.

Given that the earliest years of life can have a profound and long-lasting effect on children's ability to learn, on their health, social and emotional well-being, our investment in the future must begin by supporting children right from the start. However, social, education, and health services for families with children under three years of age are few and fragmented. In the U.S., unlike in many other industrialised nations, the family has sole responsibility for caring for infants and toddlers. But changes in the economy and in American demographics make it increasingly difficult for parents to do so. Today, parents of young children are more likely to be separated from extended family; are working more and earning less; are spending more time worrying about safe housing, affordable health care, and adequate childcare, and are spending less time with their children.

As a result, more young children are at-risk due to hurried, harried, and inconsistent lifestyles. By toddlerhood, many children have not developed the skills of the "competent" three-year-old, and by early school age as many as 35 per cent are unprepared for the demands and opportunities of kindergarten.

RISKS TO SCHOOL SUCCESS

The task of the focus group participants was to discuss problems they saw (in their practise, in the neighbourhoods, or with their own children) as early warning signs of later preschool difficulty. They were asked to restrict their discussion to problems evinced within the first three years of life. The locus of the problems could be the child (e.g., speech delay), the parent (e.g., an overprotective parent), or the environment (e.g., no opportunity for peer play). The outcome "school difficulty" was intentionally vague to maximise the range of responses and open discussion among group members.

Each focus group generated an extensive list of "early warning signs," presents several themes that were common across groups and across sites. The most striking finding is the similarity in the concerns of parents and providers. Interestingly, no one mentioned the lack of traditional pre-academic skills such as children's knowledge of numbers, letters, colours as a concern. Instead, participants in both

Fremont County and Lawndale discussed more basic issues such as the development of self-control, respect for others, a sense of confidence and competence. Their concerns were broad, ranging from aspects of parenting, the child, and the child-parent relationship to the family as a socialising agent, and the larger context of the neighbourhoods. Parents and professionals were passionate and sincere, and readily voiced their concerns for the children of their communities. The observations of providers and parents alike were astute and their illustrations were often poignant and alarming.

Despite demographic differences (viz., urban vs. rural, race and ethnic composition), Lawndale and Fremont County participants were similar in terms of their concerns. Where differences did arise, they tended to reflect a greater range of troublesome circumstances or more severe forms of the risk conditions in Lawndale. Drug abuse and gang involvement is more widespread in Lawndale and appears to be taking a particularly heavy toll on family routines and the safety of young children.

A social worker in Lawndale described just how extensively drug use can interfere with parenting—for instance, one mother routinely sold WIC foods to buy drugs and fed her infant table scraps instead. She was proud her infant never ate "baby" food and kept her in the oven of their tiny one-room apartment because she couldn't tolerate the sound of her crying. As an aside, equally alarming is that the court did not find cause to remove this baby from her mother's home. The problems of drugs and alcohol are not confined to Lawndale, however. Fremont County parents and professionals also spoke of increasing numbers of parents with alcohol problems, and babies affected by parents' alcohol and drug use.

The most unexpected finding from the focus groups was the grave concern of both parents and professionals about increasing numbers of infants and toddlers who are unsupervised and left to raise themselves. Such families were described as lacking routines and schedules. When hungry, toddlers are expected to find themselves something to eat; when sleepy, they nod off wherever they are. When asked how a lack of supervision and routine in the home bode poorly for later school success, the groups were quick to share a well-reasoned developmental sequelae.

One Fremont County mother said that lack of supervision leads to lack of respect for adults because children don't feel adults' rules are valuable or relevant. As a result, she offered, children left to raise themselves will have difficulty following rules in school and getting along with others, and are likely to end up as loners.

PROBLEMS IN INFANT AND TODDLER YEARS

Problems and Concerns: Survey participants were primary care givers of one or more children under three years of age. Demographic characteristics of participants, by site. Reflecting the racial and ethnic mix of the surrounding geographic communities, the majority of Fremont County mothers were Caucasian, and all participating Lawndale mothers were African-American. On average, respondents were in their mid-twenties, and had begun childbearing near the age of 20. Twenty-two per cent of Fremont mothers, and 40 per cent of Lawndale mothers had been, or were, teen mothers (younger than 18 years at first birth).

Thirty-one per cent of Fremont mothers and 47 per cent of Lawndale mothers had not completed high school. Only seven per cent of Fremont County mothers were single; whereas 41 per cent of Lawndale mothers were without partners. No doubt reflecting the greater earning capacity of two-parent families, proportionately more Lawndale families reported incomes of less than $9,000 per year.

The average household size was 4 persons in Fremont County and 5 persons in Lawndale. There was no significant difference in the proportion of infants (12 months) and toddlers (13 to 36 months) represented by families in the two communities. Both communities' samples contained slightly more families with a child under one year of age.

Statistical tests of differences between the two samples showed that children in Lawndale were at greater socio-economic risk due to proportionately less household income and more teen mothers, single parents, and households with four or more children. Children in Lawndale were also at greater risk due to the accumulation of stressors. That is, a greater proportion of Lawndale parents could be characterised by two or more of the following five characteristics: low income, teen birth, less than high school education, large family size, or one-adult household. Seventy-eight per cent of Lawndale families and 20 per cent of Fremont County families surveyed had two of more of these five risk factors.

Despite the social and demographic differences between Fremont County and Lawndale, parents' reports of their concerns were similar. In both communities, most concerns were about children's health and physical development (e.g., questions about feeding, sleeping, age of sitting, walking, and talking), followed by concerns about cognitive and emotional development (e.g., questions about discipline, how long to leave a baby crying, how to handle tantrums, whether to limit television viewing) and concerns about establishing and maintaining family habits and routines.

Parents in both communities were most likely to express concerns about health and physical growth (mentioned by 98 per cent of parents in Fremont County and by 85 per cent of parents in Lawndale). Next most common were concerns about cognition and emotional development (85 per cent Fremont parents; 82 per cent Lawndale parents), and then questions about family habits and routines (85 per cent Fremont parents; 77 per cent Lawndale parents). On average, parents in Fremont County described ten concerns; parents in Lawndale described nine.

Parents in the two communities were also surprisingly similar in their discussion of problems they experienced in caring for their infants and toddlers. The survey asked about demanding and defiant behaviours such as fussing, attention-seeking, and noncompliance; acting out and aggressive behaviour such as biting, kicking, and being overly active; sullen, moody, or shy behaviour; and signs of possible developmental problems such as short attention span, delayed speech, or accident proneness.

Approximately two-thirds of parents in both communities reported problems with aggressive and demanding behaviours. Just over half reported moody, dependent behaviour. One-third of parents in Lawndale and nearly half of the parents sampled in Fremont County described language, motor lags, or attention difficulties.

"Serious" Problems: Because struggles for autonomy and independence are characteristic and developmentally appropriate within this age group, it is possible that most reported "problems" were simply exaggerations of age-appropriate behaviours. Thus parents were asked, "which if any of the problems you've described are of serious concern to you?" Approximately 20 per cent of parents in both communities (a total of 23 parents) indicated that one or more problems were "serious"; most of these parents (21 of 23) described problems regarding toddler-age children.

In Fremont County, 10 of 12 parents described one serious problem and two parents described two serious problems. In Lawndale, 6 of 11 parents described one serious problem and five described two serious problems. Thirteen different problems were discussed. The most common, described by three or more parents, were child bites, kicks, or hits adults; child has temper tantrums; and child has speech or language difficulties. Most serious problems described by parents were behavioural. Four parents were seriously concerned about potential developmental problems and one parent had both behavioural and developmental concerns. The most common "serious" developmental concern, noted by five parents, was speech or language difficulty. Thus in the combined two-community sample, 16 per cent (18 of 116 parents) reported serious behaviour problems, 3 per cent (4 parents) reported serious developmental concerns, and approximately one per cent (one person) reported both.

Sources of Help and Advice: When asked for their top three "preferred and most trusted" sources of advice and support regarding their children's development, parents in both communities most frequently indicated their own, and other, parents. This finding was particularly characteristic of Lawndale parents; 95 per cent of those surveyed listed other and their own parents among their top three sources of advice. The second most common source among the top three was health care and social service professionals; the third was local Family Centre services.

Interestingly, although many children attended daycare and preschool programmes and many families included older, school-age children, relatively few (7 of 119 parents) considered education professionals among their top resources. The proportion who utilised education professionals (defined as daycare, preschool, or school teachers) was relatively higher among families with school-age children (12 per cent vs. 3 per cent) but was unrelated to whether the young sibling was of infant or toddler-age.

When asked for their number-one preferred source of advice, over half the parents surveyed in Fremont and Lawndale mentioned their own and other parents. Health and social service professionals were ranked first by 32 per cent of parents in Fremont and 18 per cent of parents in Lawndale. Family Centre services were ranked first by 10 per cent of families in Fremont and three per cent in Lawndale.

Specific Concerns and Help Sources: Over half the parents surveyed in Fremont and Lawndale had concerns regarding how to tell if their child was developing normally, how to identify physical illnesses, how much and how often to feed their children, when and how to discipline, and what to do about their child's irritability and crying. In addition to these, over half the Fremont County parents were also concerned with toilet-training, teething, how to make the child's environment hazard-free, how to help children feel secure, when their children would sleep through the night, and how to choose quality childcare.

Parents in both communities discussed a large number of concerns (N = 599, Fremont; N = 512, Lawndale), and all 22 concerns were discussed by at least 20 per cent of parents in each community (the prevalence of individual concerns ranged from 20 to 71 per cent).

Fremont parents' responses to questions regarding specific developmental concerns were somewhat incongruous with their previously stated "top" source of advice. Previously, 53 per cent selected "other parents" as their preferred source of advice and only 31 per cent selected health and social service professionals. However, specific developmental concerns were referred to these two sources almost equally.

The third most frequently endorsed source of advice was the Family Centre's services. Lawndale parents' responses more closely approximated their overall rankings. Of 512 concerns, 222 were referred to other parents and 142 were referred to health and social service professionals. Relatively few concerns were referred to the Family Centre and few sought assistance from formal parenting education (e.g., through WIC).

In Fremont, no single concern was the exclusive domain of other parents, health and social service professionals, or the Family Centre; yet the data do suggest some degree of "consumer" specificity. Questions regarding feeding, developmental ability, teething, and illness were at least three times more likely to be referred to health and/or social service professionals, whereas more personal decisions regarding feeding mode (breast or bottle), discipline, pacifiers, bedtime routines, and returning to paid employment were preferentially discussed with other parents. In Fremont, questions regarding toilet-training and the attainment of other developmental milestones were discussed equally with other parents, health and social services providers, and the Family Centre.

The pattern was slightly different among Lawndale parents. With the exception of questions regarding developmental level, parents sought the advice of other parents as often, or more often, than any other source. For example, parents with questions about childhood illnesses were just as likely to turn to other parents, as they were to seek advice from health professionals. As in Fremont, parents perceived the Family Centre's expertise to include information about toilet-training and choosing childcare.

Specific Problems and Help Sources: The three most common problems discussed by parents in Fremont and in Lawndale were temper tantrums, moodiness (is easily upset), and stubbornness. Each problem was discussed by at least one-third of parents in each community. In addition, at least 20 per cent of Fremont parents described the following problems: short attention span, sleep problems, hurting other children, child is overly active, child is fearful, child is lagging in language or speech development, and child is too demanding.

Fremont parents discussed a total of 237 problems. The most common sources of help were other parents, health and social service professionals, and the Family Centre. Problems were referred almost equally to these three sources; however, parental concerns regarding child's attention span, an indicator of possible developmental delay or behaviour disturbance, were 2.5 times as likely to be referred to other parents or the Family Centre as they were to health or social service providers.

Lawndale parents discussed a total of 230 problems. In addition to the three most common problems shared by parents in Fremont County, over 20 per cent of Lawndale parents reported problems with children hurting other children, being overly active, being too demanding, constantly seeking attention, and hitting, biting, or kicking adults. 60 per cent of all problems for which a help source was mentioned were referred to other parents.

As in Fremont County, even potential signs of developmental delay were typically referred to other parents. For example, parents who noted children's speech problems were just as likely to turn to other parents for help as to health and social service providers.

Associations between Family Characteristics and Concerns, Problems and Help Sources: A series of analyses were performed to identify relations between aspects of the family and reported concerns, problems, and parents' help-seeking behaviour. For the first set of analyses, regarding associations with socio-economic factors, a cumulative risk index was constructed of five binary variables: annual income of less than $9000, four or more children in the household, mother less than 18 years of age at first birth, mother with less than high school education, and only one adult in household. Thus, the risk index could be a number from zero (none of these risk indicators) to five (all five risk indicators) for any given family. The range was from zero to four for Fremont families, and from zero to five for Lawndale families.

Pearson correlations between family risk and number of reported concerns and problems suggested only a weak linear relationship with most variables ($r < .30$; $p > .05$), so the family risk index was dichotomised based on fewer (less than 2) vs. more (2 or more) stressors. Chi-square tests were computed to learn whether family hardship was related to perceived sources of advice and support, or to reported developmental concerns and problems.

For the most part, parents at relatively different levels of socio-economic stress reported similar help-seeking behaviour except that in families with fewer stressors, parents were more likely to include self-help efforts (e.g., reading, and observing others' children) among their resources (Chi-square = 7.08; $p < .01$). Level of socio-economic stress was not significantly related to parents' report of developmental concerns, or to the total number of concerns they discussed.

Socio-economic stress was related to the number of problems parents discussed, but in an unexpected way. In families with fewer stressors, parents reported significantly more problematic behaviours. On average, parents in the lower-stress group reported five problems; the average of the higher-stress group was three ($t >= 2.71$; $p < .01$). Analyses by problem types showed that parents in the lower-stress group reported more problems of all types; differences between the groups were statistically significant ($p < .05$) for dependent, moody behaviours and for resistant, demanding behaviours.

Results of these analyses raise two comments. First, because the absolute number of problems of each type was small (less than two problems of each type on average), the inverse relation between socio-economic stress and number of behaviour problems should be regarded with caution. One possible interpretation is that, in the absence of unrelenting family hardships such as extreme poverty and lack of adult-support, parents are more likely to identify and discuss disruptive behaviour.

Second, it must be acknowledged that Lawndale families are over-represented in the "high" risk group because, in these data, site and risk are confounded. However, the pattern of findings for the combined group is similar to that within each site, thus it seems unlikely that the noted associations with socio-economic stress are related to inherent differences between the two communities such as locality or ethnicity.

A second set of analyses examined potential differences between families whose youngest child was an infant (< 12 months) versus a toddler. The results showed no significant relation between child's age and parents' help-seeking behaviour. Similarly, there was little relation between child's age and parents' report of developmental concerns and problems; recall that most parents endorsed concerns of all types and as many as two-thirds described problems of the types probed.

Where differences were found, they were in the area of physical and intellectual development. More parents of infants expressed concerns about health and physical development and more parents of toddler-age children described potential developmental problems, though few noted they were of "serious" concern. These group differences were not statistically significant ($p < .05$).

Promoting School Success begins in Infancy: The final set of survey questions asked parents directly about early learning activities in the home. Over two-thirds of parents reported that they felt they had enough time to provide quality learning experiences in the home. The most common activities were reading, casual talking, playing, or singing, and more formal teaching of verbal routines such as prayers, names of letters and colours, child's name, and address. Understandably, given the age range of this study, few parents reported separate or scheduled learning activities such as educational outings, lessons, or structured pre-academic activities such as "Hooked On Phonics." Parents of toddlers were significantly more likely to describe skill-building activities incorporated in family routines (43 per-cent vs. 24 per cent; Chi-square = 4.76; $p <.05$).

When asked how community members could help parents prepare children to do well in school, responses ranged from parent-focused programmes (such as parent education, home-visiting programmes, etc.), to the need for better outreach regarding existing programmes, to ways of strengthening links between home and school. In addition to increasing parent involvement and knowledge of resources, both groups recommended several child-focused activities. The most popular suggestion was the provision of peer play groups. The common vision was of mixed-age groups facilitated by knowledgeable adults who would take primary responsibility for activities, but attended by parents as well. Nearly half the sample reported that providing assistance with transportation and providing evening and weekend activities would help them take greater advantage of new or existing programmes.

CHILDREN'S PROBLEM

The job promotion and move to another country was the chance of a life time. Your family was going to experience another culture, move to a new neighbourhoods, make new friends, try new foods and have your children go to different schools. It was all very exciting and you did everything you thought you needed to do to prepare your children for the upheaval. Perhaps one of your children was struggling a bit in his home school, but surely, going to a new environment and starting fresh would be just the answer you were looking for.

Fast forward to six months and reality is looking a bit different. Your eleven-year-old daughter is thriving and fitting in beautifully, but your sixteen-year-old son is struggling. You are not sure if it is simply the move and different surroundings, or if it something to be concerned about. The teachers have been calling more frequently saying that your son seems quieter than usual, that although bright, doesn't seem to be engaging in class as he did when he first enrolled. You can't imagine that he could be so quiet at school, because at home, he has been a terror. Moody, slamming doors, prickly at the slightest request to help around the house, and you find yourself capitulating to his demands simply to get some peace. The walking-on-eggshell syndrome is alive and well at your home.

Your son's school suggests that perhaps seeing a professional may smooth out some rough edges and help him over the hurdle. Concerned that something is going on with your son that may be more than simply a move from the States, you are not sure what to do, but you know something has to change.

As a first step, it is highly advisable for your child to undergo a complete battery of psycho educational testing by a psychologist trained to tease out emotional and educational issues. Good testing, which will take several hours, can reveal whether your bright son is actually struggling with some hidden learning issues. He may have been able to compensate before but now all of a sudden, the work load at school is more than he can handle. He may feel stupid, marginalised and embarrassed to admit it.

Next, find a good therapist who is used to work with adolescents. Your school may be a good first stop option for referrals. If you are fortunate, these two steps may work, and your son or daughter may be able to succeed by working with a good therapist and additional accommodations at his school to address possible learning differences.

If not, you'll need to consider other options. At this point, you might want to consider engaging an educational consultant, trained in working with struggling youth. That would involve hiring someone who has first hand knowledge of a variety of school placements, preferably from visiting personally, is not affiliated with any programme, and not receiving any compensation for placing a student in a specific school.

Examining current psychological testing, speaking with professionals who have previously worked with your child, including taking a social profile of your child, acting as a liaison for your child with the admissions director, including explaining your child's profile, visiting your child during their residence at the programme, supporting the family through the entire placement process and being available for any questions and concerns during this process, are all part of the role of a special educational consultant.

Although the U.S. educational system may lag behind in many areas, it is far ahead of other countries in recognising special needs problems and creating solutions. There are currently thousands of special programmes dealing with this population.

Options for kids who have not succeeded in traditional school settings, due to emotional/behavioural hurdles now include: therapeutic wilderness programmes, which can last from six weeks to several months and usually non-academic, re-habs for substance abuse, from twenty-eight days to three months, also usually not with an academic piece, emotional growth schools and therapeutic boarding schools, which range from a year to 18 months, residential treatment centres, which vary from nine months to a year, psychiatric hospitals for shorter term stabilisation of a couple weeks to a couple months and programmes to help over 18-year-old who may not be ready for college and need to learn how to navigate the world more successfully away from their family. The over 18-year-old programmes will vary from skills training lasting six months, to programmes integrating academics or vocational training as well as life skills and some group therapy, lasting a year to 18 months.

The rule of thumb is the more clinical the psychological profile of the child, the higher level of care required. Along with that higher level of care, comes more frequent therapy, more highly trained professionals and or psychiatrists and more cost. Children with fewer psychological issues will require a lower level of care at a lower cost. But everything should really be based on the individual needs of the child and his/her particular profile.

Simply because you heard from a friend that they had a child who went to a programme and it worked out beautifully, is not a good enough endorsement that it will work the same for your child. The therapist working with your child at the programme, the particular issues facing your child, the population at the time your child is in residence, the degree that the family is willing to participate honestly on re-learning some parenting skills and the investment that your child has that this is an opportunity to create a better future for himself, are all part of the puzzle that needs to fit together to get a favourable outcome.

Only you can decide if you feel that the investment of time, money and energy is worth making to help your child. If you feel that the problem is more with your child than with the family system, and that he can get repaired like a piece of broken crockery, the "fix" may be very temporary. However, if you decide as a family, that you are willing to learn some new tools which may help to heal your relationship with your child, there is a reasonable expectation that it may work.

The comforting thought for parents should be that if you feel that you are at the point where you need to try something else, there are many wonderful options out there for the child who is struggling.

❑

6

CAREER MAKING

For many teenagers, one of the hardest questions to answer is, "What do you want to be when you grow up?" People may seem to be asking you this question all the time. They are asking you to pick your major in college, decide where you want to go to school, decide what you want to do with your life... The question you might have is, "How the heck should I know???"

There's a funny fact of life that you should keep in mind as you think about your "career," your major in college and so on. That fact of life is this: Almost every successful adult that you see today went through a crazy and totally unplanned path to get to his or her current position in life.

Ask just about any adult who you admire and who has a great job, "How did you get where you are today?" You will see how crazy these paths can be. For example, you might know someone who has a great job as a newscaster on TV. When you ask him how he got to be a newscaster he might relate the following story to you:

"Well, when I started college I really wanted to be a geologist, but I ended up having to take a required class in computer programming. I really liked programming, so I ended up changing majors and graduated as a computer scientist. I started out working for IBM and didn't like it, and then began working for a small company. They got this project with a TV station writing software for the news room. One day I got a chance to meet the news anchor for the station and we really hit it off. He liked my voice and suggested I go to broadcasting school. I did that for two years. Then one thing led to another and now I am a news anchor myself."

If you talk to ten successful adults, nine of them will have totally unbelievable stories like this. It is absolutely normal, and it is common.

So, in choosing your own career and in picking your major, what should you do? One approach would be to simply relax, find something you like doing now, major in it in college and get a job. Then be on the lookout for new opportunities. Take them when they arise and enjoy life. That would be a completely valid approach.

Another approach would be to do some research on different career possibilities so that you can see what's out there. There are thousands of jobs that you have never even heard of before, and one of them might be perfect for you. One way to learn about them is to start asking every adult you know, "What do you do for a living?" and then "Do you like it, and why?"

BENEFITS TO TEEN WORKING

I will examine the positive impact of having your teenager work. This is an important topic because three-fourths of high school teenagers are working more than fifteen hours a week on average, and this number is steadily rising (Grant & Snyder, 1984 in Artwater, 1988). This increasing prevalence is linked to many positive affects that teenagers experience in their social, economic, and academic realms. First I will describe the positive social aspects of work that teenagers will encounter. Second, I will discuss the monetary benefit of teenagers working. Lastly I will discuss the academic advantages that working teenagers will have over the non-working teenagers.

Social Aspects of Teenagers Working: There are many positive aspects for teenagers that work during high school. Increased social skills are just one of those aspects that benefit teenagers. There have been many studies conducted on the positive social aspects a teenager acquires while being in the working world.

Most of these studies have stated that there is an increase in punctuality, dependability, and personal responsibility among teenagers (Kablaoui & Pautler, 1991). Also, a teenager will acquire more developed social skills that may impact all aspects of life such as school and ability to develop friendships or get along better with teachers, or in everyday social life with friends and the teenager's ability to interact and support their friends.

According to a study done by Finch, Mortimer, Shanahan, and Ryu (1991), found that the effects of work experience on control orientation in adolescents. They found that the quality of work (i.e., its stressful and rewarding character) is a more important determinant of adolescent psychological functioning than either work status or its intensity (Finch et al., 1991). Finch et al., (1991) also found that there was evidence suggesting that the quality of tenth-grade work experience is a source of adolescent mastery orientation for both genders.

These researchers also found that, "Complex work that requires self-directed thought has beneficial outcomes, increased adult self-confidence, self esteem, intellectual flexibility, and involvement in work; lessening anxiety and fostering self directed orientations and intrinsic occupational values" (Finch, et al., 1991). In another research article by Bailey (1992), describes what the effects are of working teenagers. Bailey (1992) found that in addition to increased spending power, youth employment is viewed as an important step between adolescence and adulthood, providing vocational experience, adding responsibilities and independence, and possibly reducing financial dependence on parents.

In this same article, the Work-Education Consortium of the National Manpower Institute in the U.S. identified eight benefits of work for youth: sustained exposure to a particular career, adult work attitudes and habits, interaction with adults, responsible behaviour, mastery of non-classroom skills and problem-solving techniques, citizenship skills and attitudes, increased academic motivation, and lifelong skills (Bailey, 1992).

The last study I found that supported development of positive social skills is by Steinberg, Fegley, & Dornbusch (1993) and discovered that in regards to work and autonomy from parents, non-workers were more closely monitored by parents and workers were granted more decision-making freedom. Also, in regards to work and internalised distress, teenagers who worked moderate hours had fewer psychological and somatic symptoms (Steinberg, et al., 1993).

Economic Aspects of Teenagers Working: There are also several economic benefits to employment for teenagers. It is stated that working teenagers have exhibited increased earning power, lowered unemployment rates after graduation, and teenagers found better jobs after graduation (Kablaoui & Pautler, 1991). In a different research article by Mortimer, Finch, Shanahan, and Ryu (1991), states that the benefits of intensive work, those who worked longer hours, had greater confidence in ability to find and keep a job after graduation.

Fortin (1996) states research done by Nicole Champagne suggests that 76.8 per cent of working teenagers want to gain job market experience from their jobs working as teenagers. Champagne asked the participants in this study, "If your parents were to give you the same amount of money you work for every week, would you go on working?" The answer was yes from 69.7 per cent of senior high school students, showing just how important young people feel their work to be. Economic factors are not necessarily the most important motive for wanting a job: sometimes young people are looking for additional training or preparation for the job market (Fortin, 1996).

Also, following is the benefits of teenagers working:

- Earn money for themselves and family expenses.
- To gain valuable time management skills.
- To gain valuable interpersonal and occupational-specific skills
- To develop discipline.
- To demonstrate responsibility.
- To enhance self-confidence and self-esteem. (Mortimer, et al., 1991)

All of these benefits stated by Fortin (1996) impact teenagers economically, and also help the teenager find and keep a job that they want after graduation.

Academic Aspects: In addition to the social and economic benefits of work, it also affects academic aspects as well for the teenager. According to Kablaoui and Pautler (1991), teenagers gain practical knowledge about the business world and have suggested that there are improved grades, school attendance and participation in school-related activities. Child and Family Canada says that the Higher Education Council has found that those who work less than ten hours a week do better at school (Fortin, 1996).

Researchers from the CECM (Montreal Catholic School Board) have shown that there is a link between time-spent studying and academic performance. They have found that school-leavers who work between five and ten hours a week get better grades. Fortin (1996) also found out the reasons from high school students of why they work (in descending order of importance):

- To develop a feeling of independence and a sense of responsibility (16.7 per cent).
- To buy clothes (16 per cent).
- To be independent of parents (10.9 per cent) (Fortin, 1996)

Among junior high school students (including those in special streams) the reasons were in descending order of importance:

- To buy more clothes (20.2 per cent).
- To develop a feeling of independence and a sense of responsibility (11.9 per cent).
- To buy a car or a motorcycle (10.1 per cent) (Fortin, 1996).

This is important in regards to academics, because there is a growing trend of teenagers going to work to make money, causing the teenager to have less time studying for school. It is interesting to see what motivates teenagers to work instead of spending that time studying.

In a research article online by the Harvard Education Letter, Research Online by Karen Kelly (1998) entitled, Working Teenagers: Do After-School Jobs Hurt?, some researchers say that the most successful job experiences are those that are closely linked to an official school programme.

Often called School-to-Work or Work-Based Learning, these partnerships between school and industry provide students with learning experiences in a real world atmosphere that can, in turn, strengthen their academic understanding (Kelly, 1998).

The majority of teenagers that work in this type of job have a more positive attitude about work and fewer academic problems than those whose jobs are not linked to a school programme (Kelly, 1998).

Conclusion: There are positives which discussed here. There are positives that affect the teenager in regards to the social, economic and academic aspects. Working helps the teenager go through this difficult time of trying to find their identity and where they fit in society.

There are also some safeguards that parents can take in making sure that their teenager has an enjoyable and gratifying experience while working according to a article entitled, Our Kids Parenting Report: Working Teens (Russo, 2002):

- Limit hours kids can work
- Grades should always come first.
- School is a job in itself.
- Teach job skills at home.

If parents implement these safeguards, then it is more likely that their teenager will succeed at school level, allowing them to have all of the positive aspects as discussed here.

CAREER'S CHOICE

Theories of how an adolescent develops career choices are a relatively new and seldom studied-phenomenon. Until recently it was assumed that adolescents underwent a natural progression, first initiated at the high school level, to the world of work. This belief was widely held until 1952 when Ginzberg introduced a developmental theory involving career choice among adolescents.

He proposed that career choice is a process which extends from about age ten to age twenty-one, and that the most important factor determining career choice is "the series of interlocked decisions the adolescent makes over time." (Adams, 1980) He further theorised that the process of career choice is largely irreversible. Generally, Ginzberg proposed that a final career choice usually resulted from a compromise between need and reality.

Influences on Choosing a Career: Ginzberg went on to identify four different ego functions that he associated with adolescents making their career choices. He found that those individuals who were more mature and able to project psychological future were better at choosing career options. The second ego function is what he called "delay function." Ginzberg defined delay function as "the ability to postpone immediate need gratification for longer term, highly-valued goals," representing what Freud called the reality principle, which produces a more realistic career choice than does the pleasure principle.

The third ego function, known as reality testing, is the process of appraising the reality of what one can do, as opposed to what one might desire to do. In other words, an adolescent may be very intellectual and talented, but may not have the financial resources to pursue a particular career. The fourth part of the ego function is an attitude of "give a little to gain a lot." Unlike other theories related to career development and identity, Ginzberg's theory unfolds and differentiates over periods and stages (Adams, 1980).

Research indicates that family background and identity is correlated with adolescent career development. Previous studies show that teenagers who reported that their mother or father was out of work tended to have higher estrangement from family members. Further, researchers have found that the break-up of parents affects identity the most. It was found that both male and female adolescents living in step-families or in single-parent families had reported higher levels of estrangement as opposed to males and females from non-divorced families (Banks et al, 1992).

Not surprisingly, the most influential roles on vocational choice include parents, peers, siblings, and school influences. Research has shown that adolescent boys who are close with their fathers tend to have more traditional sex-typed ideals about vocation. Furthermore, boys tend to follow on in their fathers' career paths. By the same token, young women who are close with their mother tend to follow in the same career path as their mother. Parents should be careful, though, not to push their kin into particular vocational directions. Research has found that parents often do not give proper advice regarding vocational choice, and therefore need to be aware of their child's identity before directing career choice (Dusek, 1987).

Peers have also been shown to affect career choice. While the effect of peers on vocational choice is dependent upon gender and social class, research indicates that boys tend to rank peer influence low when it comes to career choice. Also, there is evidence that lower-class boys who attend middle class schools tend to have higher aspirations than do lower class boys who attend lower class schools (Adams, 1980).

Siblings are also an influential factor when choosing a career path. Boys with all male siblings have been found to hold mainly masculine vocational interests, while girls with female siblings hold feminine ones. Researchers have also found that older brothers act as significant role models for younger siblings. The older brothers may also be responsible for those women who have entered traditionally masculine lifestyles (Banks et al, 1992).

Perhaps the biggest influence on vocational choice are the schools, since schools have recently been focusing more on training for occupation, than mere teaching to create more highly educated individuals. Studies have found that 39 per cent of college students regard their high school teachers as the major influence regarding their occupational choices. Guidance counsellors in schools have the ability to be highly influential when it comes to helping young teens choose a career path. Guidance counsellors should have the resources and the understanding of the student's goals in order to realistically advise the adolescent in a positive manner. Although these actions should represent the norm, there has been evidence that guidance counsellors are really not doing their best in these matters. Studies have repeatedly indicated that students feel they get little or no help from their school guidance counsellors (Dusek, 1987).

Programme for Career Decision Making: Is there any help for adolescents making career decisions? Fortunately, there is help that is known as "I-Power." Tiedemans developed the I-Power programme, the major focus of which is to increase self-direction. A major portion of the I-Power focuses on an intensive examination of present personal discussion of how teenagers maintain their current system. The results of the I-Power programme are impressive in that they found an increase in ego-development scores; an increase in the use of planned analytical decision-making strategies, a decrease in impulsive strategies, an increase in tests of critical thinking and finally, a decrease in aimless/delaying strategy. Miller-Tiedeman concluded that this type of educational programme should be a keystone of career programmes for both secondary schools and colleges.

Conclusion: Adolescents gain more freedom and responsibility with age. They have more decisions to make as they grow older. One of the biggest choices they have to make is their choice of career. Parents, families, and friends have a large impact on young adults life, especially career. With the information provided, parents will hopefully be more aware and able to help their teens navigate through the working world.

TEENS PREPARE FOR COLLEGE

It seems to be that every parents dream to have a child going to college, knowing that they will graduate as a doctor, nurse, lawyer, and businessman. Not every child is on the path to attain secondary education though. Some will not even finish high school. According to the National Centre for Education Statistics (NCES), 86.5 per cent of American teenagers are completing high school.

Others believe it is much lower because those with a GED are included in the findings. GED's are not considered equivalent to a high school diploma because students do not graduate from a high school and the demand placed on those receiving a GED is much less than that of a person receiving a diploma, although the majority of employers consider the GED to be equivalent.

Continuing Education: The best way to encourage children to continue education is to become interested in what they are doing, interact with them by providing them with the resources they need to flourish into a well-educated adult. By focusing your attention on goals achieved in school, teenagers will more likely be able to attain goals in their career choices and future. Here are some simple ways of helping your teenager on the path to success.

- Identify the goals your child has and help them to achieve those goals. The more influence you have in helping them reach their goals successfully, the more likely they will go on to secondary education.
- Support any school involvement they have. Involvement in school activities helps increase the interest they have in school. Keep them involved.
- Recognise any special needs that they have. Recognition of their needs early on can help make up for lost time in the future. If school work is too difficult , try to help them or get a tutor to help a child understand what may be unclear to them.
- If a regular school seems too much for them, think about placing them in a different school. A different school can make all the difference. Certain schools can provide the individual attention needed for each student that might otherwise be overlooked.
- Realise that not every child is cut out for college. Even if yours is, realise that realistic goals for your child should be kept in mind. Not everyone is ready to be the next astronaut. Help your child to find a major that is directed toward an interest. Finding a major that a child is happy which can make college life much easier and shorter.

The most important thing is to interact with your child, keeping the lines of communication open. This will ensure there is no confusion and that the road to educational, financial and career success will be a less than bumpy path.

Conclusion: Think about the future, knowing your children are the future and helping them decide on the best route to take will help to make life easier. Making your child have an enjoyable time in high school, helping them graduate and feeling self-confident enough to further their education will allow all to benefit from their knowledge.

BALANCING SCHOOL AND WORK

Many more teenagers now work in today's modern society than ever before. During the 1980's a sharp increase occurred in the number of teenagers who held jobs while enrolled in school. In fact, most teens worked more than twenty hours per week while still attending school.

Because more teenagers work more hours per week, they are spending significantly less time on their schoolwork. Researchers have begun to conduct studies regarding the relationship of adolescents' academic success and their maintaining jobs, as well as trying to determine whether having a job as an adolescent carries with it positive or negative effects.

Academic Success of Working Teens: One would assume that maintaining a job as an adolescent would promote positive self-identity and growth, responsibility, the development of future career goals, and higher academic expectations for him/herself (Sprinthall, 1995). Some research does indicate that teenagers who work while attending school develop more practical skills, deal more effectively with people, have an enhanced work-orientation with higher job values, and display feelings of importance (Dusek, 1987). However, most research suggests that there are negative consequences toward high school students who are employed, especially those who work more than twenty hours per week.

In the Steinberg, Fegely, and Dornbach study, the researchers were interested in determining the significant differences of academic success between adolescents who were employed and those who chose not to work while in school. Drawing upon previous research, they hypothesised that teenagers who were employed had poorer pre-employment attitudes and beliefs as opposed to their counterparts, the teens that did not work. They began by surveying high school students living in Wisconsin and northern California during the 1987-1988 and 1988-1989 school years.

They administered surveys to the participants at the beginning and end of each school year to compare the two groups of students. They found that the students who eventually found employment (held no jobs during the first survey, but became employed by the second) had lower grades and lower future educational expectations, spent less time on homework, and were more likely to be disengaged from school activities than the non-working students. However, they did not find a difference in pre-employment attitude regarding class effort, skipping classes, mind wandering, classroom attention, or classroom concentration (1993).

From the second evaluation the researchers also found that non-workers developed significantly more positive school profiles; yet, those students who left the labour force demonstrated better school performance. No significant difference in classroom effort, classroom concentration, or school orientation between the two groups could be determined. However, the researchers found the most negative orientation towards school came from those adolescents who decreased the hours they worked, while the most positive orientation toward school came from the students who left the labour force (1993).

Overall, the Steinberg, Fegley, and Dornbusch research provided significant evidence that adolescents who are employed while enrolled in school become less engaged in school-related activities. Furthermore, teenagers who work more than twenty hours per week are more likely to demonstrate a lower degree of investment in their educational programmes. Finally, these researchers found that teenagers, who leave the work force while they are students, are more likely to regain improvement in school performance (1993).

Researchers Steinberg, Greenberger, and Garduque (1995) have found that teenagers who hold jobs are more likely to be absent from school and enjoy school less, than those students who are not employed. Steinberg, Greenberger, and Garduque also indicate that working adolescents experience less time in extracurricular activities. Moreover, they additionally suggest that working teens promote the predominant cultural view of adolescent society, which includes a longer period of time with less responsibility and more discontinuity in the healthy attainment of adulthood.

Teenagers who work are likely to be employed in the retail and food service fields. While these areas provide good jobs for teenagers, these jobs do not help increase their cognitive abilities. Furthermore, these jobs do not help teenagers to develop long range occupational and or future educational plans (Dusek, 1987).

Greenberger and Steinberg studied 3,000 Los Angeles teenagers from a wide range of socio-economic backgrounds in order to be able to apply their research findings to the vast majority of teenagers in the nation. They found that two-thirds of all sixteen year-olds worked part-time.

In addition, they discovered that teenage employment is distinct to our culture in that the average student spends almost the same amount of time in class (21 hours) as at a job (25 hours). Like other researchers, Steinberg and Greenberger also found negative relationships between being employed and maintaining high academic levels. Interestingly, they found that students who held jobs were more likely to persuade their teachers to lower the course requirements. In addition, these students were more likely to have higher amounts of tardiness, to lie about incomplete homework, and to become more tolerant of cheating. Furthermore, the researchers found little evidence of teenagers gaining maturity, developing responsibility or displaying insight from having had an occupation.

Conclusion: Concerned with the negative aspects associated with school and employment, Steinberg and Greenberger hypothesised reasons for the negative aspects of the working students. They feel that isolating teenagers in age-segregated jobs, where the nature of the job itself requires almost no training, is not conducive to positive educative experiences. Moreover, they believe that the general ethics in places of employment such as food services and retail establishments, are not conducive to teaching basic values of responsibility and character (Dusek, 1897).

Although it seems likely that adolescents who are employed would be more responsible and would have defined their future goals, this does not appear to be the case. From the research that has been conducted, it is apparent that there are many costs associated with teenagers who are employed. However, there are situations in which teenagers must work in order to supplement their family income and, therefore, do take their jobs more seriously than academics. I believe that each adolescent needs to have a healthy balance of part-time employment and school-related activities, and be able to fully realise the benefits of one without ignoring the other, in order to become successful in life.

HOW WORKING PARENTS AFFECT TEENS?

It is extremely common this day and age to find families in which both the mother and the father are employed. Females are tending to get married at a later age and therefore, have children when they are older because they want to pursue their careers. This also coincides with the idea that after a woman does have a child, she eventually goes back to her job. If a mother and father are both working, who is raising their children?

What does that child do while their parents are working? Does having these working parents affect the child developmentally? These are all questions and concerns that parents may have when they are working and raising adolescent teens simultaneously. This section of the book is intended to answer these questions and provide parents with information that will help them to better understand their own specific working situation.

Concerns: It has become an all-to-familiar scene with the recent phenomena of teen violence. Instances of shootings, such as the one in Columbine, have made many wonders if parental involvement is non-existent these days (Shellenberger, 2000). How could these things happen, not to mention happen over and over? It is a common belief that if parents were to pay more attention on their kids, this would never happen.

However, parents have become seemingly obsessed, focusing all their attentions to their careers, and leaving little attention for their children often out of economic necessity. Parents seem to have the feeling that once their child is old enough to stay home alone by themselves, they are then grown and the parents work is done. This, however, is not the case because adolescence is a time of critical growth.

"Millions of school-age children in the United States get out of school each day before their parents get home from work (Belle, 1999)". What these children do in these hours of solitude may be unknown to their parents. Some participate in after school programmes, some are looked after by others, but many are by themselves (Belle, 1999). It is this relationship between working parents and their children that may ultimately lead to struggling, troubled teens (Shellenberger, 2000). These teens may become rebellious and unruly.

Parents play a major role in the development of their children and when their focus is not all present, their teens tend to do things to make them pay attention. Teens become disobedient and defiant based on the lack of attention and care that they naturally crave at this stage in their lives. This, in turn, creates a hostile home environment. "Many working parents of troubled teens are finding family problems like theirs are surprisingly common (Shellenberger, 2000)".

This however, establishes more trouble because unlike problems that are associated with younger children, problems with teens are not widely acceptable reasons to be distracted from work or other like priorities (Shellenberger, 2000). Adolescents do not want to let on that they need their parents, but they in fact do. Parents are slowly but surely realising that they need to change how they are balancing work and their family life, because in the end, their adolescent teens are the ones who are suffering the most.

Solutions: "Now work-and-family specialists see growing interest in career adjustments that allow parents to keep closer tabs on teens (Gardner, 2000)". Parents are realising that their adolescent children need more supervision than they had been previously receiving. This may mean coming home from work earlier or creating special meeting times to talk (Gardner, 2000). They are also realising that just because their child is older does not necessarily mean that their job of raising their child is done. Adolescents may say that they do not want there parents to come to a special event, that it "doesn't really matter", but in actuality the teen is thrilled when the parent takes off from work and takes the time to spend with them.

Working adults are finding that the period of adolescents is one of the most crucial and critical as well, and it is during this time that teens struggle with their own identity. They are coming into a period of maturation and development that is scary and uncertain. They need guidance and strong support features that come from their parents (Gardner, 2000). Adolescents need their parent's reassurance and direction to help them form other normal, functioning relationships and healthy ideals.

"More parents are also asking for work-place seminars on parenting teens. At employees' request, employers are booking 50 per cent more information sessions on adolescent issues than a year ago (Shellenberger, 2000)". Parents are realising the importance of their involvement with their teens. They have come to an understanding that they are in fact able to work, but that this means their adolescents require some extra care and attention. They realise that they must give their children more "focussed" time (Lewis, 1999). Closer supervision and parental involvement are also instrumental in guiding their teens along the right path.

Conclusion: It has become a trend for parents to both be holding down careers and a household simultaneously. This is true in both households with two parents, and especially in single-parent households. This may be because of the increasing rate of females wanting to have their own career or simply because the family is struggling financially, and needs two incomes to stay alive (Lewis, 1999). No matter what the reason may be, it almost always has an affect on the couple's teen. Working parents are dividing their attention between their career and their adolescent, and in many cases the one that suffers is the adolescent.

A working parent is prone to become over-worked, stressed out and chronically tired. This all leads to a lack of focus on their home-life. When a working parent comes home, many times they are to exhausted, mentally and physically, to devote the needed amount of their attention to their adolescent.

Concerns arise when these teens become deviant, which in many cases they are apt to do. Parents are now coming to the realisation that their careers do have an affect on their child, because this period of adolescence is one of critical growth. Now more than ever, these parents are asking for help from the workplace in order to put the focus back onto the lives of their children.

They understand that it is possible to posses both a career and raise a family, but they are now recognising that there is work to be done in both areas. There has been literature that supports the idea that balancing time and focusing energy when need be, is important for the healthy development of their teen.

Careers in: Speech Language Pathology

Speech-language pathologists (SLPs), or speech therapists as they are often called, work with people who have difficulties talking or swallowing. They evaluate and treat a wide variety of problems related to speech and language, including problems stemming from disease, injury, development disabilities and birth defects.

SLPs also work with people who wish to modify or eliminate accents, stop stuttering, improve their communication skills or to alter the tone or pitch of their voices. Speech therapists use their skills in government or corporate positions doing research or developing speech-loss prevention programmes.

Unless they are conducting research or developing programmes, SLPs work directly with clients on a one-to-one basis. To assess problems, they use written or oral tests as well as special instruments to record and analyse speech difficulties. To treat patients, they develop an appropriate treatment plan, which they may pass along to another SLP or implement themselves.

Some SLPs work independently, providing services to clients in a private clinic or office setting in much the same way as other medical specialists. They work with individuals or can set up contract arrangements with institutions such as schools, hospitals and elder care facilities. Others work as staff people in medical facilities and work as part of a team of doctors, social workers, psychologists and other therapists.

How to Succeed?: To be happy and successful in their work, SLPs must be patient and detail-oriented. In some cases, a patient might be capable of only limited (or no) improvement despite months or years of therapy. SLPs must be willing to put in the time to document cases thoroughly, especially long-term cases that require substantial insurance reimbursement.

A typical day for an SLP employed on staff at a major medical facility might include a staff meeting, meetings with other practitioners to discuss specific cases, evaluating a head trauma patient, and counselling a patient with multiple sclerosis on what changes he can expect in his speech capabilities as the disease progresses.

An SLP who works for a school system might spend the day travelling from school to school to discuss suspected speech problems of special needs students with teachers or setting up and conducting evaluations of students. Part of the day might be spent reviewing or updating individual treatment plans for students with speech difficulties.

In private practice, the SLP could spend an hour or two coaching someone with a speech impediment or accent on how to pronounce specific sounds, then travel in the afternoon to a nursing facility to visit clients there. An SLP who works in research might be involved in an evaluation programme for a new computerised hearing aid or analysing data from a multiple-client study.

Career Outlook: According to the Federal government's Bureau of Labour Statistics (BLS), about 94,000 people held jobs as SLPs in 2002. About half of these people worked for, or in, educational institutions including public schools, colleges and universities. Most of the others worked in clinical settings inside of hospitals or nursing homes or provided services through health care facilities such as outpatient or home health care centres, and a few worked in private practice.

The Bureau estimates that employment prospects for SLPs will grow faster than the average job growth rate through the year 2012. The average annual growth rate for all jobs is less than two per cent, but that figure takes into account jobs that are disappearing. The BLS says that health-care related employment opportunities are among the fastest growing areas of employment.

Information gathered from state labour projection organisations estimates that about 5,000 new SLP positions will open between now and 2012, plus people will be needed to fill existing slots as people retire or leave the field for other reasons. The states with the biggest percentage change are Nevada, Utah and Idaho, followed by many of the Southern states. According to these figures, all of the percentage increases are double-digit with a maximum of 49 per cent in Nevada.

You can easily understand that anyone involved in working with the elderly will find increased job opportunities as the Baby Boom generation continues to get older. As people age, they can experience problems with their hearing for several reasons, including strokes. SLPs will find ample opportunities to work with older people during the next several decades.

The BLS also expects SLP job opportunities to open up within elementary and secondary school systems as more children are evaluated for disabilities. Federal law guarantees that all children with special needs receive appropriate evaluation and treatment, including children with speech-related disabilities.

In addition, children with attention-deficit disorder often have some sort of speech-related-disability such as auditory processing problems (difficulties in understanding spoken speech). These children can also benefit from working with SLPs.

SLPs with dual or multiple language proficiencies should find ample work opportunities serving communities or areas where multiple languages are spoken routinely. Medical service providers in such areas are finding it difficult to adequately provide for the needs of the population. According to information published in Advance, a magazine for SLP professionals, the Hispanic population has increased 300 per cent in Georgia during the last decade.

Within ten states in the South, the Hispanic population has increased almost 200 per cent on average during that time. SLPs who are bilingual in Spanish and English should find increased job opportunities working in all settings in these areas.

Pay Day: Annual salaries for SLPs are less than those of general medical practitioners or medical specialists, but the earnings are respectable. Plus, SLPs are seldom asked to work nights and weekends or long shifts. Typical working hours are office hours and a normal work-week is 35 to 40 hours with no on-call work.

The BLS latest compensation figures are from 2002 and indicate that on average SLPs earned about $50,000 that year. The middle range (50 per cent) earned anywhere from $39,930 to $60,190. The highest salaries were about $75,000 and the lowest about $33,000. SLPs who worked with other health practitioners or in medical environments made more on average than SLPs who worked in elementary or secondary schools-about six thousand dollars a year more.

The American Speech-Language-Hearing Association (ASHA), one of the biggest associations for SLPs, conducted a salary survey of its members in 2003 that gives more detail about SLP compensation. According to the survey, the median salary for full-time certified SLPs who worked year-round (as opposed to working on an academic year basis) was $48,000. SLPs who worked nine to ten months and in academic settings made slightly less, about $44,800.

These figures are national averages and represent all experience levels. They will be lower in less-populated areas and lower all around for people who are starting their careers. The ASHA's survey indicated that the national average for starting salaries for people with one to three years of experience was $42,000 for those who worked on a calendar-year basis and $37,000 for those who worked on an academic year basis.

Education and Training: To work as an SLP, you will need a graduate or doctorate in a related doctrine; usually people start with a graduate degree in speech-language pathology. Some people who work as SLPs have graduate degrees in audiology or speech-language science.

You don't need an undergraduate degree in SLP to get into an appropriate graduate programme, but you do need a bachelor's degree, and having a major in a related health field is a definite plus. A programme with an emphasis or a major in communication sciences and disorders or communicative disorders is an excellent foundation for later SLP education and training.

If you are interested in a programme with an emphasis in minority issues or a bilingual focus, the ASHA site contains a list of programmes run by Historically Black Colleges and Universities, as well as minority/bilingual emphasis programmes.

For example, San Jos State University's graduate programme in SLP is one of the programmes listed on the ASHA Website, and information on the University's Website explains how SJSU interprets and implements diversity in the programme: "The programme curriculum integrates the various aspects of diversity and its corresponding issues, including practical information regarding working in a multicultural environment, communicating effectively with interpreter/translators, and interacting with clients from a variety of cultural and linguistic backgrounds in hospitals, schools, clinics, and the department's on-campus clinic."

Two more examples are Washington State University, which has an SLP programme with an emphasis on working with Native Americans, and Florida International University, which offers a bilingual speciality track in its SLP graduate degree programmes with such courses as Cultural and Linguistic Diversity in Communication Disorders and Assessing the Bilingual Child with Communication Disorders.

The Council of Academic Programmes in Communication Sciences and Disorders maintains its own list of undergraduate and advanced degree programmes in SLP in the United States, Canada, Puerto Rico and New Zealand.

If certification is important to you, then you need to have a degree from an ASHA certified programme, so read through the information on the list carefully. This list is organised by name and by state/location.

Expand Your Horizons: While you are working on your undergraduate degree, look for opportunities to expand your education beyond the classroom. You will be able to put theory into practice, and you will be better able to evaluate if you want to pursue a career in working with people with speech difficulties.

Participate in hands-on work as much as possible even if the only opportunity in a clinical setting is to observe or to handle paperwork. People pursuing a graduate degree in speech-language pathology must make a greater effort to do clinical work because experience is part of the certification requirement.

Students can gain experience through summer internships or even volunteer work. ASHA runs summer camps around the country for people (especially children and teens) with speech difficulties and is always looking for people to help at the camps.

If you are working on an undergraduate degree in communication sciences and disorders and decide not to pursue an SLP-related advance degree, you can still put the degree to use.

You can work as a SLP aide or assistant. Assistants must be supervised by SLPs, but under their guidance may be allowed to perform many of the evaluations and execute treatment plans. State regulations govern what aides can and can't do and regulations do vary.

You do not need a bachelor's degree to work as an aide (a two-year degree from a technical school in SLP is enough in some states) although employers do typically prefer a bachelor's degree. As an aide, you also don't need to be certified or continue your education through course work beyond your degree. SLP aides with several years of experience make about 60 per cent to 70 per cent of what an SLP with comparable experience would earn.

Licensing and Certification: To be a full SLP, you must (in most states) obtain a license and part of the licensing requirement is an applicable master's degree. You will also be required to pass a Praxis exam and a national exam on SLP, which is offered by the Educational Testing Service. A certification from a major industry association such as ASHA may also be required.

Other requirements include several hundred hours of supervised clinical experience and nine months of postgraduate professional clinical experience. To keep a license current, 38 states require ongoing education to earn continuing education credits. Most private health insurance companies require practitioners to be licensed to qualify for payments, as do Medicare and Medicaid.

The ASHA certification programme offers certificates of clinical competence (CCCs) that are recognised and accepted nationwide. In some states, a CCC is all you need to satisfy that state's SLP licensing requirements, and in most states the CCC is one of the requirements. To gain the certification, you will need to have passed the Praxis exam, gained the hundred hours of clinical experience, and have accumulated the necessary continuing education credits from an ASHA-approved CE provider or through approved independent study. Re-certification is necessary every three years.

While still in school, you should consider becoming a member of the National Student Speech Language and Hearing Association (NSSLHA). To join, you must be a student enrolled in a part- or full-time degree programme related to communication disorders. When you join you have access to print journals and profession-related discounts. Most important of all, membership gives you access to invaluable networking opportunities that will make it much easier to get experience while you're in school and land a job when you're completed your studies.

Related Professions: SLPs often work with other health care professionals such as medical doctors and psychologists. However, the closest related health-care occupations to SLPs are audiologists and speech language and hearing scientists. Audiologists work with people who have hearing or balance disorders. Some people have speech and hearing problems, requiring the expertise of audiologists and SLPs.

The training, experience, certification requirements and day-to-day work duties of an audiologist are similar to those on an SLP-with the exception of the nature of the problems the client exhibits. Audiologists also make about as much money as SLPs.

A speech, language and hearing (SLH) scientist needs a research doctorate degree in a related doctrine. Certification is not required to conduct research, but some scientists do acquire the relevant ASHA certification.

SLH scientists usually pick an aspect of the discipline to focus their research efforts. Within this area of focus, they spend their time researching biological, physical and physiological communication processes. Or, they spend their time researching the psychological or social effects of SLH disorders on affected individuals. Usually, these scientists work in a university or college environment, but some do private research funded by corporations.

Sound Benefits: Becoming a degreed professional in the SLP field gives you the opportunity to have a satisfying career helping others while you earn a first-rate salary. The top earning prospects go to those who have graduate and doctorate degrees, but even someone with the appropriate two-year degree can gain entry to the field.

Demand for SLPs will increase during the next decade and in some areas demand will exceed supply; experienced licensed practitioners can look forward to having their choice of job opportunities. Continuing education requirements and re-certification are a must for those who remain in the field more than a few years, but this slight disadvantage is outweighed by the bright outlook and career opportunities that abound in this exciting field.

ROLE OF ELECTRONICS

Teens today have so much more to distract them besides their homework, the opposite sex, friends, family members, and extracurricular activities. Besides learning how to drive, teenagers are occupied with playing with an assortment of electronic gizmos including cell phones, camera phones, personal computers, MP3 players, DVD players, ipods, xboxs, digital cameras, the list goes on. Wired? You betcha...and then some. Perhaps all of this electronic gadgetry has you concerned and you are wondering just how you can extract your teen and involve them in an outside activity where they can expand their minds and refresh their bodies. Are you out of ideas? Let's look at some options that may appeal to them and remove the worry from you.

Work on the Car: So, you think that a car isn't a kid magnet as much as when you first learned how to drive? Think again. Today, kids are *pimping their rides* and expressing themselves through their cars. Custom paint, decals, blacked-out windows, even faux aircraft wings are being attached to the outside of their cars. On the inside, it can be totally surreal: rear view mirrors wrapped with a studded belts, frilly seat cover trim, pushpin art attached to the headliner, decals everywhere, etc. Let them pimp your Camry or Explorer...that'll keep them off the computer...and get you noticed too!

Volunteer: Help your teen organise a group of his or her friends to clean up the neighbourhoods, paint an elderly neighbour's house, teach younger kids how to ride bikes, or visit folks at the local nursing home. You remember when you were a teen and you heard the comments from your parent's generation about kids not wanting to do anything or being "no good," right? With a little direction, young people can do just about anything and are more than willing to help out if you believe in them. Rewards are nice too...be prepared to throw a pizza party after their time of service is over for the day.

Get a Job: Kids who hold a job while going to school learn how to handle their money and budget their time. Limit work hours to lesser than 20 per week to ensure that their grades are not adversely affected. If your student is involved in extracurricular activities too, make sure that this time is included with the hours that they work. Maintaining good grades is essential, no job or outside activity is worth it if it takes away from their schooling.

In all cases, show your teen that you believe in him or her. As you know, parenting is much more than providing for their needs...you want to guide your child from youth toward adulthood by showing them that there is much more to life than all things electronic. So, gently disconnect your teen and get them involved with other pursuits.

Making the Summer Camp Decision: The thought of 'summer camp' can evoke strong emotions on the part of parents and children alike. These emotions run the spectrum from excitement and fun to fear and anxiety. Camp isn't for everyone—child or parent. In many social circles it is a status symbol or a family tradition. Neither of these reasons are the appropriate reason for sending your child to camp. The correct reason for providing the 'camp experience' is if it is 'in the best interest of the child.'

Deciding to camp or not to camp—in the best interest of the child is all well and good, but how does a parent determine what is 'in the best interest of the child?' Some questions parents can ask are:

1. Is the camp being used to solve a childcare problem?
2. Is this an opportunity for my child to learn, grow and experience life in a unique way?
3. Is my child adventuresome—a risk taker?
4. Does my child enjoy new experiences; is she ready to do new things when, or even before I am ready to provide them?
5. Has my child enjoyed overnight experiences with family or friends?
6. Does my child have friends and/or cousins who attend camp?
7. Will camp provide opportunities for my child to enjoy favourite activities?

If you answered 'yes' to questions two through seven you have it made. If you answered 'yes' to question one only, the odds of success are slim. If you answered 'yes' to at least four of questions two through seven, the odds are optimal for a successful camp experience.

Selecting the right camp—the 'right' camp is the one that supports the interests of your child. Select three or four camps that have activities that interest your child. Visit these camps without your child to determine if they meet your specifications. Some important issues are: the ratio of camper to counsellors, the training and experience of the counsellors, medical facilities (especially if your child has on going medical needs). Check food, diet and menus. Are there choices of activities? Ask for references.

After you have narrowed it down to two or three camps, take your child to visit and allow him/her to choose which camp she likes best. Allowing your child to choose is crucial for success. You do not have to decide quickly. Indeed, beware of the camp management which wants a decision quickly.

If your child is reluctant to commit to a camp, gentle encouragement is usually the key in dealing with a reluctant camper. This is probably not the first time your child was reluctant to do something new. What is she concerned about? Listen, but do not tell your child that it will be okay or that you can protect him/her—because you won't be there and that may be the core of the concern. Acknowledge the concern or fear as valid. Children usually have a solution to their own problems. Through careful questioning, allow your child to find the answers. Talk about a similar experience and how it was solved, and the possibility that the new situation could be solved in the same manner.

Your child wants to camp, but you may have concerns. Be careful not to convey your concerns. Avoid phrases like: "Don't worry about..." Call the camp and state your concerns and rely on your reaction to their response. However, having done your investigation earlier, you really would have only minor doubts.

There remains the possibility that your child did not have a good experience last year and therefore does not want to attend this year; or, positive experience notwithstanding, your child is reluctant. Start at the beginning as if it were the first time. Ask yourself the seven questions, research camps, visit, select and gently encourage. Sometimes parents need to make an executive decision. In the best interest of the child you may need to make an empathetic, supportive, but not popular decision. After a second negative experience in a different camp, consider, however your child just may not be a camp enthusiast.

One last consideration—your child may voice reluctance to go, or complain about the food, activities, etc. because she is afraid that showing eagerness to go and/or 'having a ball' will make the parents feel rejected. Reassure your child that you will miss him/her, but remind your child, "I am glad you have a good time at camp.' More often than not you will have a happy camper.

❑❑

32. Baby Names for Girls **(New)** 125/-
33. Baby Names for Boys **(New)** 125/-
34. Art of Public Speaking 125/-
35. The World's Greatest Speeches 125/-
36. Group Discussions 110/-
37. Personality Development 110/-
38. Think Positive & Things Will Go Right 110/-
39. Once in a Blue Moon (A Tantra Tale) 125/-
40. God is Dead 125/-
41. Travel India (A Complete Guide for Tourists) 295/-
42. Glimpses of Urdu Poetry 450/-
43. Indian Mythology 195/-
44. How to Reduce Tension 125/-
45. A Book of Stenography 150/-
46. Business Letters 125/-
47. Baby Names for the Boy 95/-
48. Baby Names for the Girl 95/-
49. Non Vegetarian Delights 125/-
50. Pure Vegetarian Delights 125/-

Lotus PRESS

Unit No. 220, 2nd Floor, 4735/22, Prakash Deep Building,
Ansari Road, Darya Ganj, New Delhi- 110002
Ph.: 32903912, 23280047, 9811594448
E-mail : lotuspress1984@gmail.com, www.lotuspress.co.in